A Revolutionary War Road Trip on US Route 4

**Spend a Revolutionary Day Along
One of America's Most Historic Routes**

OTHER REVOLUTIONARY WAR ROAD TRIPS

by Raymond C. Houghton

A Revolutionary War Road Trip on US Route 7
(Pittsfield, MA to Burlington, VT)

A Revolutionary War Road Trip on US Route 9W
(New York City to Kingston, NY)

A Revolutionary War Road Trip on US Route 9
(Kings Ferry, NY to Saratoga Springs, NY)

A Revolutionary War Road Trip on US Route 202
(Elks Neck, MD to Philadelphia, PA)

A Revolutionary War Boat Trip on the Champlain Canal
(Bethlehem, NY to Champlain Maritime Museum, VT)

A Revolutionary War Road Trip on US Route 20
(Albany, NY to Boston, MA, in preparation)

A Revolutionary War Road Trip on US Route 60
(Charlottesville, VA to Yorktown, VA, in preparation)

A Revolutionary War Road Trip on the Mohawk Turnpike
(Oswego, NY to Schenectady, NY, in preparation)

A Revolutionary War Road Trip on US Route 221
(Chesnee, SC to Augusta, GA, in preparation)

A Revolutionary War Road Trip on US Route 4

**Spend a Revolutionary Day Along
One of America's Most Historic Routes**

Raymond C. Houghton

Cyber Haus
Delmar, NY

A Revolutionary War Road Trip on US Route 4
**Spend a Revolutionary Day Along
One of America's Most Historic Routes**

Revolutionary War Road Trips
are published by Cyber Haus
and printed on-demand
by Booksurge, LLC,
www.booksurge.com,
1-866-308-6235.

ISBN: 1-931373-09-4

Cyber Haus
159 Delaware Avenue, #145
Delmar, NY 12054
www.revolutionaryday.com
www.cyhaus.com
cyhaus@msn.com
518-478-9798

**To my wife Jan
and all travelers
who can't pass
a historical marker
along our most
historic highways!**

INTRODUCTION

US Route 4 goes from Portsmouth, NH to Albany, NY, but for its last 100 miles you can find much history – history that dates back to three very important years in the United States' struggle for independence: 1775, 1776 and 1777. This book presents a one-day, road trip along this route, but be warned, with so much to see, it could easily take a week.

In 1777, British General Bur-goyne described this area as "God Forsaken", but he no doubt was frustrated by the stubbornness of its citizens who would not surrender to his invading army. Actually, this area covers some of the most beautiful country in the northeast. It's no wonder that its citizens would not give it away.

A Revolutionary War Road Trip on US Route 4 begins early in the morning in Castleton, Vermont, historically on May 9, 1775 when final plans were being made for the capture of Fort Ticonderoga. Throughout the day, you will detour from Route 4 several times, including one big detour at the beginning that goes about 20 miles to the north. This detour sets the historical stage for the last 100 miles on US Route 4.

From Castleton you will cross Route 4 and head north on the old military road through the Hubbardton Battlefield and Mount Independence, then cross Lake Champlain by ferry to Fort Ticonderoga

and Mount Defiance where on July 4, 1777, Burgoyne moved cannons up to the top of the mountain and sparked an American retreat from Fort Ticonderoga and Mount Independence.

You will continue south following the route taken by the British during the invasion of 1777 through Whitehall, Fort Ann, Fort Edward, Fort Miller and Schuylerville following the Hudson River to the Saratoga National Historical Park where the battles of Saratoga took place, the "turning point of the American Revolution."

From the park, you will continue south following the Hudson River through Stillwater, Waterford and Peebles Island until you complete your journey in Albany, the target of the British invasion and home of General Philip Schuyler, the commander of the Northern Department of the Continental Army.

So, if you're ready, begin your **Revolutionary Day** along historic US Route 4.

A Revolutionary War Road Trip on US Route 4

TABLE OF CONTENTS & TRIP LOG

xii

CASTLETON

Castleton was a crossroad during the American Revolution. On July 6-7, 1777, Major General Arthur St. Clair and about 2,500 American troops encamped near Castleton. The troops were retreating from British pursuit that began at Fort Ticonderoga the day before. The American troops would move through Castleton and then travel east to Rutland,  then turn south to Manchester and finally head southwest to Fort Miller. Just south of Fort Miller, they would be reinforced and defeat the British at the Battles of Saratoga.

Two years earlier in May 1775, Ethan Allen, Seth Warner, Edward Mott, John Brown and Benedict Arnold and a force of about 250 American troops encamped here at the farm of Richard Bentley. They were here to make final plans to seize Fort Ticonderoga from the British. George Washington needed the cannon and munitions held at Fort Ticonderoga for the siege of Boston.

Ethan Allen and Seth Warner had about 200 Green Mountain Boys from Vermont. Edward Mott had about 16 Connecticut men. John Brown had about 40 men from the Berkshire Mountains of Massachusetts. Colonel Benedict Arnold from Connecticut brought a commissioning from the

Massachusetts Committee of Safety. Since this was the first time Americans were considering an offensive action against the British, they were no doubt risking their very lives.

Their plan was for a small party to move west to Skenesborough to capture boats from Major Philip Skene, the great Tory landholder of the region. The boats would then be used to cross Lake Champlain. Ethan Allen would go north ahead of the group to spy out the land near Fort Ticonderoga. The main body would rendezvous with Ethan Allen later that evening. They would then cross Lake Champlain under the cover of darkness and surprise the British in the morning.

The place where the meeting took place is marked in Castleton. Between the Birdseye Diner and the congregational church, you will see what looks like a veterans memorial with American flags flying. This "memorial" is actually a large stone that marks the meeting place.

Breakfast in Castleton – Have breakfast at the Birdseye Diner. Be sure to ask what the breakfast special is.

While you're having breakfast at the diner, remember that not far from this very spot in May of 1775, Ethan Allen, Seth Warner, Edward Mott, John Brown and Benedict Arnold had breakfast at the farm of Richard Bentley.

Fort Warren – Just down the road at the intersection with East Hubbardton Road (a half-mile east on Route 4A), you will find two markers for Fort Warren and the American retreat. Both markers indicate that Fort Warren stood on this site from 1777-1779. After the loss of Fort Ticonderoga and Mount Independence, Fort Warren became a part of a string of forts built across the state for the defense of Vermont. North of these forts all the way to Canada became a demilitarized zone. Those that remained in or entered the area did so at their own risk.

FORT WARREN

**Battle of Hubbardton
7 Miles North**

Directly east is the elevation for Fort Warren built in 1779 for defense of the Northern Frontier. The road from the north was the route of American retreat before Burgoyne protected by Colonel Seth Warner's rear guard action at the Battle of Hubbardton, July 7, 1777.

(Castleton Marker)

CASTLETON TO THE
HUBBARDTON BATTLEFIELD

Mile Mark 0.0 – Turn left onto East Hubbardton Road and head up this old military road to the Hubbardton Battlefield.

Mile Mark 0.2 – Crossover over US Route 4 and continue going north.

In the 1700's, this road was used by the Americans to get back and forth from Mount Independence and Fort Ticonderoga on Lake Champlain.

This is a curvy road that goes up hills and through farms. You will see lots of trees and lots of cows (Rumor has it that there are more cows than people in Vermont). Trees are something the British were not used to — most of the trees in Britain were cut down long before the Revolution. America was like the Vietnam jungle to the British. Americans used the trees for cover and to build fortifications.

Mile Mark 4.6 – There are no markers between Castleton and the Hubbardton Battlefield, but there should be one about two miles south of the battlefield. It is here where General St. Clair and his forces were encamped when they heard gunshots that marked the beginning of the Battle of Hubbardton. It was the early morning hours of July 7, 1777. They broke camp quickly and were in Castleton just a few hours later.

Arthur St. Clair
by C. W. Peale

East Hubbardton road becomes Monument Hill Road as you approach the battlefield. As you climb the road you will reach an open field on the top of the hill.

Mile Mark 6.6 – Arrival at Hubbardton Battlefield.

THE HUBBARDTON BATTLEFIELD

The battlefield area is encircled by a walking trail that is about a half-mile in length. Along the trail are several markers that describe the battle and mark positions of the American and British Forces.

The Visitor Center is open from 9:30 AM to 5:30 PM, but the site can be toured before the center opens. The center contains a museum and a three-dimensional relief map with fiber optics.

The Battle of Hubbardton – American Major General Arthur St. Clair, retreating from Fort Ticonderoga and Mount Independence, had left at Hubbardton about 1000 men to form a rear guard. Through this maneuver, St. Clair was not only able to escape after the British arrived with his weary and tattered main army, but he also stopped the pursuing forces in their tracks.

Battle of Hubbardton

Only battlefield on Vermont soil. Here on July 7, 1777 a successful rear guard action by Col. Seth Warner's Vermont, Massachusetts, and New Hampshire troops ended British pursuit under General Fraser and Riedesel. Thus General St. Clair's American Army retreating from Fort Ticonderoga and Mount Independence was saved to fight again near Bennington and Saratoga. Burgoyne's 1777 drive to divide the colonies first resisted at Hubbardton ended in defeat at Saratoga.

(Hubbardton Battlefield

The American forces at Hubbardton were comprised of Vermont's Colonel Seth Warner with a detachment of Green Mountain Boys; a detail of Massachusetts militia under Colonel Ebenezer Francis; and Colonel Nathan Hale commanding the 2nd New Hampshire Continental Regiment.

The pursuing British units of Lieutenant General John Burgoyne's Army were seasoned regulars. Some 850 men were led by Brigadier General Simon Fraser, one of Burgoyne's best line officers. Fraser was ably supported by a detachment of 200 or so Brunswick troops under Major General Baron von Riedesel, a competent field officer.

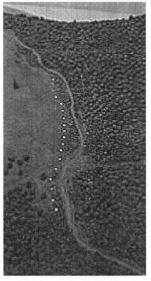

About dawn, on the morning of the Battle, the stage was set: The British pursued the retreating Americans along the old military road from Mount Independence to Hubbardton. The course of the road is still clearly visible on the hillside across the valley from Monument Hill.

As the British column reached Sucker Brook, the Americans were attacked. The Americans then retreated to positions atop Monument Hill, a good spot for a defensive action. The British deployed and attacked the hill, but were immediately repulsed and even pursued in their retreat to their former position.

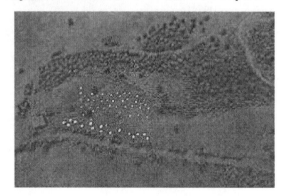

The Americans returned to the hilltop and again the British attacked and were repulsed. Thus the Battle continued for over an hour as the British attempted to flank the American defense. They, in turn, retreated to positions on the fence line east of the Military Road.

At this point the Brunswick troops under von Riedesel reached the scene and immediately attacked the American right with fixed bayonets, band blaring and drums drumming. American Colonel Francis received a mortal wound during the Brunswick attack. By this time, General St. Clair's troops had safely reached Castleton and the American troops could withdraw.

Although the American's were defeated, they had actually done precisely what was required in a rear guard action. They had fought the fully deployed enemy to a standstill and had given their main force time to move on. They had done so with skill and courage. Warner's men left the field with a great moral victory.

The Battle of Hubbardton involved about 2,000 troops and resulted in a total of about 600 casualties, or roughly 30 percent of all

Col. Warner commanded.

Col. Frances was killed.

Col. Hale was captured.

The Green Mountain Boys fought bravely. The only battle fought in Vermont during the revolution on July 7, 1777.

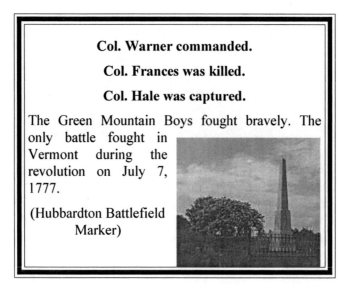

(Hubbardton Battlefield Marker)

participating troops. The losses were approximately equal on both sides.

The Hubbardton Battlefield Monument – The monument was erected in 1859. It is constructed from Vermont marble and surrounded by a cast iron fence. The monument marks the place where Colonel Ebenezer Francis is believed to be buried.

The leadership qualities and bravery under fire, shown by Colonels Warner and Francis during the conflict, had earned the highest respect of their adversaries. General von Riedesel, a veteran of many European campaigns, had especially admired these two youthful American officers. When Francis' body was found after the battle, Baron von Riedesel personally saw to it that this gallant young Colonel received a Christian burial, with full military honors rendered by a detachment from the Brunswick troops.

HUBBARDTON BATTLEFIELD TO MOUNT INDEPENDENCE

Mile Mark 6.6 – From the battlefield, continue north on Monument Road. Although this is not a major highway, it will eventually connect with Vermont Route 30.

Mile Mark 8.8 – Don't panic! Monument Road becomes a dirt road for a couple miles, but it's a hard packed dirt road, not even close to the conditions in 1777. The road does narrow a little as you go through a mountain pass.

Mile Mark 9.8 – Relax, the road returns to a welcome black tar once again.

Mile Mark 10.8 – Note the view off to the right of your car. On a clear day you can see down into the valley. Lake Hortonia is off in the distance on the valley floor.

Mile Mark 12.2 – Monument Road ends at a stop sign. Turn right. This is Vermont Route 30 heading north.

Mile Mark 13.8 – Lake Hortonia is on the left as you drive along its eastern bank. It's a very picturesque lake with many lake homes on the western bank. Keep an eye out for slow moving milk trucks.

Mile Mark 15.5 – As you enter Sudbury, watch for views of Champlain Valley off in the distance as you come down the mountain.

Mile Mark 18.5 – A sign on the left provides directions to Mount Independence. Turn left onto Route 73 West, also the route to the Ticonderoga Ferry to New York.

Mile Mark 23.7 – Travel through the scenic town of Orwell, which is centered around the church, as many small New England towns are.

Mile Mark 23.9 – You will reach the intersection with Route 22A. Diagonally across the intersection is a military road marker. Travel across the intersection and continue following Vermont Route 73 West.

Mile Mark 24.2 – Watch for the sign to Mount Independence on the left. Bear left at this intersection. Once again, you are off the major highway and prepare for another dirt road in a few miles.

Mile Mark 25.7 – Pass a farmhouse on the right at the top of a hill. As you travel down the hill, note the views

> ### Mount Independence Military Road
>
> Route to Hubbardton, 1777. After Ethan Allen seized Fort Ticonderoga in 1775, the Americans built a floating bridge from Fort Ticonderoga to Mount Independence completing the Military Road. Following Burgoyne's invasion, General St. Clair evacuated the forts, retreating down this road and across these hills to Hubbardton.
>
> (Route 22A Marker)

of Lake Champlain in the distance and Mount Defiance on the far side of the lake.

Mile Mark 26.0 – Watch for a stone, Military Road marker on the right at the bottom of the hill and the American Flags that surround the marker.

Mile Mark 27.2 – The road splits. Bear right to Mount Independence. The left fork leads down to Chipman's Point on the lake.

Mile Mark 27.7 – Note that you are now clearly on a penninsula with views of Lake Champlain on the right

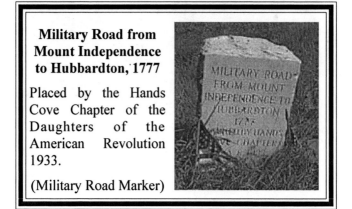

> ### Military Road from Mount Independence to Hubbardton, 1777
>
> Placed by the Hands Cove Chapter of the Daughters of the American Revolution 1933.
>
> (Military Road Marker)

and East Creek on the left. The high ground to the front is Mount Independence with Mount Defiance behind.

Mile Mark 28.2 – Pass right through the middle of Audet's Lake Home Farm.

Mile Mark 28.6 – The road returns to dirt as you drive along the east bank of Lake Champlain. Watch for the split. Bear left up to Mount Independence

Mile Mark 29.1 – Arrive at the Mount Independence Visitor Center.

MOUNT INDEPENDENCE

Mount Independence is designated a National Historic Landmark. The site is covered by several miles of hiking trails that wind past the remnants of batteries, blockhouses, hospital, barracks, and other archaeological remnants of this once-bustling fort complex. In the Visitor Center Museum, the story of military life atop the Mount is told in exhibits featuring

Mount Independence

In 1776, General Philip Schuyler identified this peninsula together with the old French fort across the narrows as the critical choke point for preventing the British from invading from the north. From July 1776 to July 1777, thousands of Americans garrisoned this site and Fort Ticonderoga. Just as construction of new artillery batteries was beginning here, news arrived that the Continental Congress declared independence. On July 28, 1776, Colonel Arthur St. Clair, the American brigade commander, read the Declaration of Independence to the assembled soldiers. After that day, East Point or Rattlesnake Hill, as this strategic height of land had been called, became known as Mount Independence. In July 1777, Burgoyne's British army forced the American troops to abandon this position. After the American evacuation, the British army garrisoned the mount and continued work on the buildings and fortifications until November 1777 following the defeat of Burgoyne's army at Saratoga. The British rearguard burned all of the structures, abandoned the site and retreated to Canada.

(Mount Independence Marker)

many of the artifacts recovered during archaeological digs.

The four trails pass through nearly four hundred acres of pasture and woodlands with vistas overlooking Lake Champlain and the surrounding countryside. Each of the trails is color-coded, but if you don't pay careful attention, you can easily miss a turn and head-off in the wrong direction.

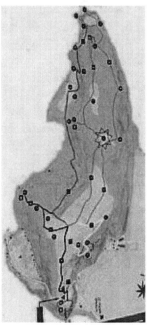

The Fort on Mount Independence – In the summer of 1776, atop this rugged hill along the shore of Lake Champlain, American troops began building this fort complex to guard against a British attack from Canada. The troops named it Mount Independence in honor of the Declaration of Independence.

Unlike Fort Ticonderoga across the lake, the fort

Exploring Mount Independence

As you explore the site, try to imagine a very different landscape during the fateful years 1776-1777. Today, Mount Independence is covered with trees and empty of structures of human habitation. During the American Revolution, the mount was a bare promontory on which all the trees had been cut. For sixteen months, it was alive with activity. Thousands of soldiers constructed fortifications and buildings with desperate haste. They lived in tents, huts and barracks, coped with miserable weather and disease, and prepared to meet the enemy. During the Revolutionary War, hundreds of soldiers from America, Britain and Germany died here from combat wounds, disease, poor diet and exposure. These dead lie in unmarked graves. Please remember their sacrifice by respecting the site. Do not search for artifacts or degrade the site. Enjoy the historical and natural beauty of this place. Leave it in the same condition for future visitors. Four marked trails lead you to the primary sites. A brochure is available to help you learn about the history of the site.

(Mount Independence Marker)

mainly consisted of huts and houses. A large shore battery and a horseshoe-shaped battery were completed. A picket fort was under construction.

As expected, the British did lead a counterattack in 1776. But thanks to delays caused by a fleet of naval ships under the command of Benedict Arnold and the combined impressive sight of Mount Independence and Fort Ticonderoga, British General Guy Carleton retreated to Canada, abandoning an attempted invasion

that year. The very next year, 1777, the opposite would occur.

Many American troops went home the winter of 1776-1777, reducing the force from 12,000 to just 2,500. Those remaining spent a horrible winter at Mount Independence. Many were sickly and a number froze to death.

In the spring of 1777, a few troops returned but not enough to properly garrison the forts. On July 5th, they evacuated the site when British General John Burgoyne's forces numbering about 8,000 began a penetration of the area. The evacuation was triggered by the astonishing placement of cannon on Mount Defiance. Fort Ticonderoga and Mount Independence

Mount Independence
Bastion of the Revolutionary War

Fortification was begun in June of 1776 and the name, Mount Independence, was bestowed following the Declaration of Independence. Lieutenant Colonel Jeduthan Baldwin was the chief construction engineer. Here the exhausted American Army, Northern Department, was stationed after withdrawing from its disastrous Canadian campaign. Built on a rocky plateau and stoutly fortified, the post was a natural stronghold facing any approaching foe from the north. Within its rugged confines, thousands of New Englanders, many succumbing to illness and lack of supplies, were quartered. Because of its commanding position and formidable battle works which made it more powerful at the moment than impaired Ticonderoga, it checked for a year, a British thrust southward until the fall of its companion fortress across the channel. It was evacuated in the early morning darkness, July 6, 1777. This critical year of reprieve gave the American forces time to organize farther south, meet and destroy General Burgoyne at Saratoga. French support eventually subdued General Cornwallis fulfilling the prophesy of the mountain's name.

Erected by the Vermont Society Sons of the American Revolution in observance of the Bicentennial of Independence, 1976.

(Mount Independence Marker)

were supposedly easy targets from the top of Mount Defiance.

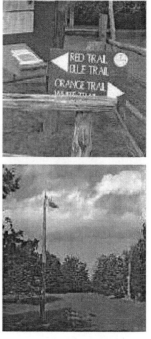

As the Americans retreated, the British pursued them down the old military road, but were halted at Hubbard ton.

The Orange Trail – This trail is the longest trail at Mount Independence and takes the better part of an hour to complete if you don't take the battery loop. Not taking the loop shortens the trail about a half-mile. All the trails are recommended on a longer visit to the area.

The old military road leads to the beginning of all the trails. The orange trail continues to follow the road all the way out to the tip of the peninsula.

Station 1 – **Barracks**. The barracks were inside the picket fort or Star Fort that was the most imposing stronghold on Mount Independence. The fort was

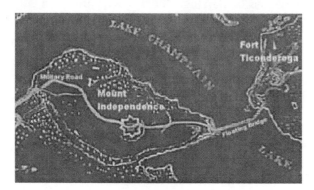

located at the highest point on the mount. The parade-ground clearing is still square, marked by cedars that have grown up along the lines of the barracks walls.

The trail meanders through some swampy areas on the mount. You can usually find boards on the ground or, in one case, a small bridge to get you across these areas.

Station 2 – Crane. The crane that was at this location was used to lift cannon, heavy equipment and supplies from the lower shore 200 feet below. The loads were carried up a ramp from boats docked in the bay below. There is a warning sign: "Caution, High Cliffs. Use Care at Mast Point." From the "mast point," there is a

Picket Fort, October 1776

Here on the highest point of Mount Independence, the Americans built a picket fort in the shape of an eight-pointed star. Inside the wooden walls were barracks, grounds and a powder magazine. Abatis defenses, constructed of felled trees pointed out-ward towards the enemy, protected the perimeter of the fort.

(Mount Independence Marker)

terrific view of Lake Champlain with Mount Defiance in the background. But also, you can see where the LaChute River empties into Lake Champlain. Fort Ticonderoga is clearly visible to the right.

At the base of Mount Defiance is Route 22 and train tracks that are used by Amtrak trains from New York City to Montreal. The area is very quiet, except for the whistle of an occasional passing train.

Station 3 – Articifers' Shops. Articifers shops are those for blacksmiths, armorers, rope makers, wheelwrights, turners, shingle makers and others with indispensable skills. There is a sign on a tree that marks Station 3, but other than that, there are no physical remains that indicate where the shops actually were at this location.

Station 4 – Horseshoe Battery. Horseshoe-shaped earthen walls enclose what was once a crescent-shaped gun platform. Inside this area is a stone memorial that

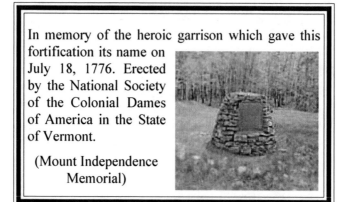

In memory of the heroic garrison which gave this fortification its name on July 18, 1776. Erected by the National Society of the Colonial Dames of America in the State of Vermont.

(Mount Independence Memorial)

was placed here by the Society of the Colonial Dames in 1963. The memorial is located where a Revolutionary War flagpole once stood. Cannon at this position commanded the lake to the north and the narrows separating Fort Ticonderoga from Mount Independence. This fortification is believed to be, at least in part, the work of Polish patriot Thaddeus Kosciuszko, chief engineer at Saratoga and West Point.

Back on the orange trail near station 4 is the intersection with the blue trail, the orange trail loop, and the returning orange trail. The orange trail loop winds around the tip of the peninsula. If you choose to take the loop, you will see Station 5 – Shore Battery, Station 6 – Bridge Site and Station 7 – Masting Point. All of these stations are located near the tip of the peninsula.

The shore battery was an extensive battery that guarded the vulnerable north shore with numerous cannon. The bridge site is at the end of a slope that leads down to the lake. The former floating bridge connected Mount Independence to Fort Ticonderoga. The bridge was 12 feet wide and was anchored to 22 sunken piers that have long since decayed and disappeared from the water.

The masting point is an outcropping of rock that is believed to be the spot where masts for boats in Arnold's fleet were stepped. The straight drop from this height into the water supports this theory.

The climb back up to the intersection with the orange trail loop and the outgoing orange trail is somewhat of a physical challenge. One can only imagine what a challenge it must have been when poorly shod, American troops from Fort Ticonderoga retreated across the floating bridge under the cover of darkness with a full set of gear on July 5, 1777.

Station 8 – Observation Shelter. At the time of the revolution, this shelter would have had a commanding view of the East Creek.

Mount Independence

Memorial to the brave soldiers buried here from 1775 to 1784 in unmarked graves and to the military importance of this mount in the War of the Revolution.

Mount Independence, named by troops camped here where they first received word of the Declaration of Independence, July 18, 1776.

Erected by the Hand's Cove Chapter of the Daughters of the American Revolution, 1908.

(Mount Independence Memorial)

Station 9 – Foundation. This rectangular foundation may have been a blockhouse overlooking East Creek. It is about 200 feet east of the stockade wall of the Star Fort.

The orange trail continues back to the military road, which leads back to the Visitor Center.

MOUNT INDEPENDENCE
TO FORT TICONDEROGA

Mile Mark 29.1 – Depart Mount Independence and return back to Vermont Route 73.

Mile Mark 33.5 – Cross over East Creek.

Mile Mark 33.8 – Reach the intersection with Vermont Route 73. Turn left and continue going west.

Mile Mark 37.8 – Norton's Gallery is on the left. Behind the gallery, you can see the area where the old military road once crossed Lake Champlain. Fort Ticonderoga is on the right; Mount Defiance is in the center on the far side of Lake Champlain. Mount Independence is on the left.

Mile Mark 39.0 – Reach the end of Route 73 and the intersection with Vermont Route 74. Turn left on Route 74 and go west.

Mile Mark 39.6 – Reach the Fort Ticonderoga Ferry, established in 1759. The ferry is actually a barge on cables that is driven back and forth across the lake. This is somewhat in keeping with the floating bridge that once crossed from Mount Independence to Fort Ticonderoga.

On the ferry's side rail is a historical marker about the landing of General Burgoyne's forces.

In late June 1777, General John Burgoyne prepared to lay siege to Fort Ticonderoga. He landed nearly 4,000 British regulars at Four Mile Point where the paper mill is now located. An additional 3,000 German mercenaries landed on the Vermont shore. Burgoyne expected to face the Gibraltar of the North, but brutal winter weather and a shortage of supplies had taken a terrible toll on the American troops defending these positions. When the British placed cannons atop Mount Defiance, American forces abandoned both Fort Ticonderoga and Mount Independence to the British and made a strategic retreat southward.

(Ticonderoga Ferry Marker)

41

After driving off the ferry, continue following NY Route 74 going west.

Mile Mark 40.6 – Watch for the entrance gate to Fort Ticonderoga on the left. Go through the gate and enter the Carillon Battlefield. The Carillon Battlefield is where the French and the British battled for control of Fort Ticonderoga during the French and Indian War. Most of the markers in the battlefield relate to this time-period.

However, there are two Revolutionary War markers. Watch for the Hut Marker on the right. Americans prepared to do battle with

Hut Sites

Within a radius of 1/2 mile were 150 huts occupied by American troops in the Revolution, 1776-1777.

(Carillon Battlefield Marker)

Through this place passed General Henry Knox in the winter of 1775 -1776 to deliver to General George Washington at Cambridge the train of artillery from Fort Ticonderoga used to force the British Army to evacuate Boston.

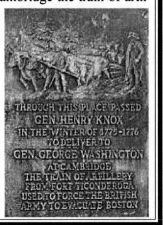

Erected by the State of New York during the sesquentenial of the American Revolution.

(Carillon Battlefield Marker)

the British on the Carillon Battlefield in 1776 and 1777.

The other marker is a "Knox Trail" maker. In the winter of 1776-1777, Henry Knox led a transportation unit to carry artillery captured at Fort Ticonderoga to Boston in order to force the British from the city. The route he traveled is called the Knox Trail. Trail markers appear at many locations along US Route 4 on the way to Albany and along US Route 20 on the way to Boston.

Mile Mark 41.6 – Arrive at Fort Ticonderoga.

FORT TICONDEROGA

When you arrive at Fort Ticonderoga, you step back in time. Fort Ticonderoga has been restored back to its original condition when the French first built the fort in 1755. To add to the realism, there are people dressed in period costume. There are also firing demonstrations and performances on the parade ground. There is always something going on to make a visit even more memorable.

In the fort's museum, you will find personal possessions of many of the major players, such as Ethan Allen and John Brown. For example, there is Ethan Allen's gun with his name engraved on the stock that he lent to Benedict Arnold. There are also many maps, three-dimensional models, historical documents and revolutionary war art.

Near the visitor's entrance to Fort Ticonderoga, there is a welcoming marker. Missing from the marker is the

Historic New York
Fort Ticonderoga

During the 18th century, when nations fought to control the strategic route between the St. Lawrence River in Canada and the Hudson River to the south, the fortification overlooking the outlet of Lake George into Lake Champlain was called "a key to continent."

The French constructed here in 1755 the stronghold they named Carillon and made it a base to attack their English rivals. In 1758, Carillon, under Marquis de Montcalm, withstood assault by superior British Forces. The next year, Jeffery Amherst's troops captured Carillon and forced the French to retreat from Lake Champlain. The British renamed the fortress Fort Ticonderoga.

During the American Revolution, Ethan Allen and the Green Mountain Boys captured Ticonderoga in a surprise attack, May 10, 1775. Cannon hauled from Ticonderoga to Boston helped George Washington drive the British from that city. In July 1777, General Burgoyne's invading army overwhelmed the American fort and Ticonderoga became British. Americans unsuccessfully attacked the fort in September 1777; later the British abandoned it.

In 1816, William Ferris Pell acquired the fort. His descendants began its restoration and in 1909 opened Ticonderoga to the public. Now the Fort Ticonderoga Association maintains the historic fort and its museum.

(Fort Ticonderoga Marker)

YEAR	HELD BY	BESET BY	RESULT
1758	French	British	French
1759	French	British	British
1775	British	Americans	Americans
1776	Americans	British	Americans
1777	Americans	British	British
1777	British	Americans	British

incredible uniqueness of Fort Ticonderoga. No fort in the world has had such an active, yet short history. In two decades, Fort Ticonderoga was the center of attack by great nations as many as six times, four times during the American Revolution.

1775 Attack – In the early morning hours of May 10, 1775, Ethan Allen and Benedict Arnold advanced upon Fort Ticonderoga with only half of their small army of about 200 due to a shortage of crossing space. The

The Capture of Fort Ticonderoga

By Alonzo Chappel

boats that were supposed to be captured from Skenesborough had not arrived in time. The group approached the fort that was being held by a small British company of about twenty men under the command of Captain Delaplace.

They marched on the fort in column, three abreast. A sentry on guard at the entrance attempted to fire at the intruders, but his gun misfired (a common problem even today — firing demonstrations held at the fort often misfire). The Americans stormed into the fort and Ethan Allen demanded surrender. When Captain Delaplace asked under whose authority, Allen responded, "the Great Jehovah and the Continental Congress." Delaplace surrendered and Ethan Allen and Benedict Arnold had taken the fort without firing a shot.

The surrender of Fort Ticonderoga marked the first overt military action by Americans against the British in their quest for American independence. It was no doubt a daring and courageous act.

1776 Attack – In October of 1776, the British, led by Sir Guy Carleton, advanced against the Americans at Fort Ticonderoga. Under the command of General Horatio Gates and the support and leadership of Philip Schuyler, the Americans were well dug-in and prepared for the British. After scouting the area and observing the impressive state of readiness at both Ticonderoga and Mount Independence, the British

changed their minds. With a coming winter and not enough time to mount a major and timely offensive, the British retreated back to Canada. They would have arrived earlier, but they were delayed by Benedict Arnold's annoying American Navy on Lake Champlain. So, after just a few minor skirmishes, the two armies disengaged until next year.

First 1777 Attack – In 1777, the British, led by General John Burgoyne, arrived plenty early enough on July 2nd and, this time, the American fortifications were not nearly as impressive. George Washington had turned his attention to Pennsylvania and did not expect the British to launch another major offensive against Fort Ticonderoga. It was the Americans who were not ready for a major offensive this time.

On July 4, 1777, British forces were observed moving cannons up the side of Mount Defiance, an action that the Americans were not prepared for. From Mount Defiance, the defenses of both Fort Ticonderoga and Mount Independence were considered relatively easy targets. So, it was decided in a council of war on July 5th

John Burgoyne
By S.Hollyer

48

that General Arthur St. Clair would lead the Americans in retreat under the cover of darkness down the military road to Castleton. When the British discovered the American retreat, Burgoyne sent a detachment to pursue  the Americans, but they were stopped at Hubbardton.

Second 1777 Attack – Burgoyne continued down Lake Champlain toward Albany leaving behind a detachment of about 200 men at Fort Ticonderoga. In September of 1777, Americans marched back to Fort Ticonderoga under the command of Colonel John Brown (the same John Brown who helped plan the capture of Ticonderoga in 1775 at Castleton). Despite outnumbering the British five-to-one and essentially surrounding the fort and even targeting Fort Ticonderoga with cannon from the top of Mount Defiance, the British forces did not retreat or surrender. The Americans had no desire to storm the walls of Fort Ticonderoga. As a result, the British held Fort Ticonderoga and controlled Lake Champlain for the remainder of the war.

Log House Restaurant – Before you leave Fort Ticonderoga, be sure to get lunch at the Log House Restaurant. It is a rustic restaurant with windows that have as picturesque a view of Lake Champlain as the fort does.

The Log House Restaurant has a couple specialty sandwiches on the menu that you might want to consider:

The Burgoyne – Grilled chicken, ham, Swiss cheese,

Dijon mustard, lettuce and tomato on a roll.

The Ethan Allen – Grilled chicken, Swiss cheese, bacon, lettuce and tomato on a roll.

If it's a really nice day, you may want to get the sand-wiches to-go and take them to the top of Mount Defi-ance, the next stop on your **Revolutionary Day**.

FORT TICONDEROGA TO
MOUNT DEFIANCE

Mile Mark 41.6 – Depart Fort Ticonderoga.

Mile Mark 42.5 – At the entrance gate, turn left onto NY Route 74 going west.

Mile Mark 42.9 – Reach the intersection with NY Route 22. Continue going straight through the intersection.

Mile Mark 43.1 – Cross the LaChute River. On the left side of the bridge is a marker; also on the side of the bridge is a memorial park that includes a Knox Trail Marker.

Carillon Bridge

Near this spot in 1755-1756, Michel de Chartier de Lotbinière, engineer of Fort Carillon, bridged this stream and harnessed this waterpower for the first time. Sawmills, storehouses and barracks were located here, being within the Seignory of Alainville granted by France in 1758 to Lotbinière. This was the first patent covering the site of Ticonderoga. His vast estate subsequently granted to British soldiers, Lotbinière in 1776 refused England's offer of compensation, preferring to aid Franklin in obtaining French support for the American cause.

Because of this sacrifice, unrequited by the Continental Congress, this bridge is gratefully dedicated to the Seignior of Alainville who was also an American patriot.

Erected by Ticonderoga Chapter D.A. R. and the State of New York, 1933.

(Ticonderoga Marker)

Mile Mark 43.4 – As you approach the Village of Ti-conderoga, look to your right and you will see a park and a waterfall. This drop is the last part of a 230-foot drop that the two-mile, LaChute River makes from Lake George to Lake Champlain. The French originally named Fort Ticonderoga, Fort Carillon due to the wa-terfalls on this river. They sounded like a carillon as the water gurgled its way to Lake Champlain.

Mile Mark 43.6 – Watch for the "grand carry" marker on the left. Just after the marker, turn right onto Tower Avenue.

Mile Mark 43.7 – Cross over the LaChute River and come to a stop at the intersection with Burgoyne Ave-nue. There are two historical markers along Tower Avenue on the right. Both have to do with the French

This tablet marks the landing for the grand carry on the great war trail between the Indian tribes of the north and south country. It also marks the beginning of that carry between the lakes to avoid the falls and rapids which later became the military road built by the French in 1755.

The French saw mill, the first ever built in the Champlain Valley was erected in 1756 at the foot of the falls on the site of the present mills. In this saw mill, Abercromby, had his headquarters during his disastrous battle with Montcalm's forces at the French lines, July 8, 1758.

Washington and Franklin passed over this military road during the Revolution.

Presented to the Ticonderoga Society for the citizens of the town by the Ticonderoga Pulp Paper Company. Unveiled by the New York State Historical Association, October 4, 1910.

(Ticonderoga Marker)

Sawmill that once stood at this site, but the one near the intersection of Burgoyne Avenue also mentions the nearby Revolutionary War fortification at Mount Hope.

Riviere de LaChute

At these lower falls stood the sawmill used in 1755 by the French to build Fort Carillon, and by the British in 1759 to build a fleet and the forts at Ticonderoga and Crown Point.

Ticonderoga Historical Society

(Ticonderoga Marker)

Turn left on Burgoyne Avenue and head up the hill to Mount Hope.

In 1756, the French erected a mill on the river opposite this spot for sawing and preparing timbers used in Fort Carillon, renamed Fort Ticonderoga when captured by General Amherst in 1759.

General Abercromby used the saw mill as his headquarters during the famous battle between the French and English, July 8, 1758, the day of his disastrous defeat; and the famous old military road, over which his army marched, passed at or near this spot and through the present mill yard.

The hill to the northwest fortified by the French and called Mill Heights, was again fortified by General Burgoyne in 1777 and called Mount Hope, its present name.

Erected July 6, 1909, by the Joseph Dixon Crucible Company, Jersey City, N. J.

(Ticonderoga Marker)

> On hill above, Mount Hope Battery, occupied by General Burgoyne 1777.
>
> N. Y. State Historical Marker 1927
>
> (Ticonderoga Marker)

Mile Mark 44.1 – Reach the Mount Hope Cemetery. Just before the cemetery is a gate and a marker. If you go through the gate, the road takes you back to some remains of the Mount Hope fortifications and a limited view towards the Fort Ticonderoga area.

Mile Mark 44.3 – Reach the intersection with Mount Hope Avenue. Turn left and head back to town.

Mile Mark 44.8 – Follow Mount Hope Avenue onto Wiley and Schuyler Streets until you reach the light at the intersection with Montcalm Street.

Mile Mark 45.0 – Turn right on Montcalm Street heading west.

> These defenses were built by American troops in 1776 and occupied by General Burgoyne in 1777 controlling the portage and lower landing place.
>
> State Education Department 1932
>
> (Ticonderoga Marker)

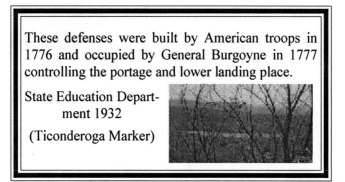

Mile Mark 45.3 – Reach a rotary with a monument in the middle. The monument recognizes Ticonderoga as a "Key to the Continent." The prominent building on the rotary is the Ticonderoga Historical Society.

After yielding to traffic in the rotary, go about three-quarters of the way around the rotary and turn right onto Lord Howe Street. It was near this street that Lord Howe was killed during the French and Indian War.

Mile Mark 46.1 – Watch for waterfalls of the LaChute River on the left.

Mile Mark 46.2 – Turn left onto Alexandria Street and cross over the LaChute River. To the right is a view of Lake George. Just after the bridge on the left is a Stoughton marker. He was the first English patentee at Ticonderoga in 1764.

Mile Mark 46.6 – Reach an intersection with Water Street; turn right. Pass Tin Pan Alley and watch for Lake George on the right.

Mile Mark 46.9 – Reach the intersection with a road simply called Portage. This road is appropriately named because it was a carrying route between Lake

Along this street ran the

Old Military Road

Fortified in 1759 by General Amherst prior to his siege of Fort Ticonderoga.

(Ticonderoga Marker)

Champlain and Lake George. After the Americans retreated from Fort Ticonderoga, Burgoyne set up his supply route along this road, a route that would eventually stretch all the way from Canada to Fort Miller on today's US Route 4.

Mile Mark 47.3 – Watch for a Military Road marker on the left.

Mile Mark 47.6 – Reach the intersection with Defiance Street. There is a Mount Defiance marker on the right. Turn right onto Defiance Street and don't be deterred by the dead-end sign a few blocks up the street.

Mount Defiance

Cannon placed on the summit of Mt. Defiance by British Artillery Officers under Burgoyne July, 1777 forced evacuation of Ft. Ticonderoga.

Ticonderoga Historical Society

(Ticonderoga Marker)

Mile Mark 48.0 – After the dead-end sign, bear right at the entrance to Mount Defiance. There is a welcome sign at the entrance with the following warning: "The road may be too steep and narrow for bus and RV's. Please watch for foot traffic."

Mile Mark 48.8 – On the left is the first set of cannons on the mountain. American troops began their retreat when they saw cannons being moved up Mount Defiance. This is also the first of many breathtaking overlooks from the mountain.

Mile Mark 49.0 – Reach the parking lot at the top of the mountain.

Two historic waterways converge at Ticonderoga. Long before the region became important to European powers, Native Americans made a portage here for carrying canoes and gear between Lake George and Lake Champlain. The two mile long LaChute River flows out of Lake George, (behind the mountain to your left), and joins Lake Champlain in the estuary below. The river, whose name means "the falls" in French, powered a French sawmill during construction of For Carillon (renamed Ticonderoga by the British in 1759) in the mid-18th century, and an impressive array of mills and factories in the 19th century.

(Mount Defiance Marker)

MOUNT DEFIANCE

Mount Defiance is open during the day from spring to fall. There is a pavilion on the top with picnic tables and many historical markers.

The road to the top is the road that was cut by the British when they observed on July 2, 1777 that the American positions at Fort Ticonderoga and Mount Independence might be vulnerable from this mountaintop. On July 4th, the American forces began to panic when they saw the cannons being moved up the mountain. The retreat began in darkness on the evening of July 5th.

In September of 1777, it was America's turn to put can-

The Fort Ticonderoga peninsula reaches east towards Mount Independence on the Vermont shore to form a choke point. Here, two waterways from the south converge, flowing north to the Saint Lawrence River. Whoever controlled this passage controlled travel between New York and Nouvelle France (Canada). American troops connected the two fortified positions the winter of 1776-1777. East Creek, on the far side of Mount Independence, protected retreating American troops from a flanking German attack in July of 1777, allowing them to regroup and fight again at Hubbardton and Bennington.

(Mount Defiance Marker)

nons on top of this mountain. Under the leadership of Colonel John Brown, cannons were placed and fired, however, the British forces did not panic, retreat or surrender. Actually, Brown found that fort was not an easy target from the mountain. The attempt to bombard Fort Ticonderoga from Mount Defiance was not successful and the British held the fort until the end of the war.

MOUNT DEFIANCE TO SKENESBOROUGH (TODAY'S WHITEHALL)

Mile Mark 49.0 – Depart Mount Defiance.

Mile Mark 50.2 – Reach the intersection with the road called Portage. Turn right on Portage.

Mile Mark 50.4 – Reach the intersection with Champlain Avenue. Bear right onto Champlain.

Mile Mark 50.5 – Reach the intersection with NY Route 74 and complete a loop around the village of Ticonderoga. Turn right at the intersection going east.

Mile Mark 51.1 – Reach the intersection with Route 22. Turn right onto 22 heading south to Whitehall.

Mile Mark 51.2 – Cross the LaChute River for the last time. Just past the bridge on the left is a marker about the river.

Mile Mark 52.6 – As you pass the Old Fort View Inn on the right, look back and you will see a parting view of Fort Ticonderoga. The mountain to your left on the other side of the lake is Mount Independence – the very place you were standing just a few hours ago.

61

> ## LaChute River
> ## Town of Ticonderoga
>
> French military engineers chose this strategic spot to build Fort Carillon to protect French Canada from the British because two water transportation routes from the south met here where the waters of Lake George meet those of Lake Champlain. The Mount Independence peninsula in Vermont nearly touches Ticonderoga point on the New York side. In the 19th Century, the LaChute River powered dozens of industries as its water fell 230 feet over a two mile course. Today a nature trail and scenic park provide access to the river. An extensive marsh behind the railroad causeway attracts many species of migratory birds in the spring and fall.
>
> (Ticonderoga Marker)

Mile Mark 58.4 – On the left is an overlook with a scenic view north, up the Champlain Valley.

Mile Mark 62.2 – Watch out for the Fox crossing the road at this spot.

Mile Mark 68.4 – On the left is another scenic overlook.

Mile Mark 72.1 – As you get close to Whitehall, cross the bridge over the southern end of Lake Champlain.

Mile Mark 74.2 – Turn left at the light onto Saunders Street then turn right on Main Street, the next intersection, and find a parking place.

Arrive in Whitehall

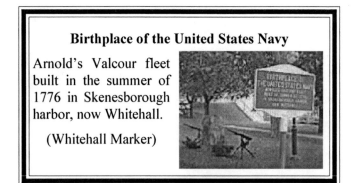
SKENESBOROUGH
(TODAY'S WHITEHALL, NY)

On the corner of Saunders and Main Streets is a park on the Champlain Canal. The canal connects Lake Champlain with the Hudson River at Fort Edward, an upcoming stop on this **Revolutionary Day**. Near the center of the park is a Navy birthplace marker. Just down the road on the left is the Skenesborough Museum. Near the museum, there is a Whitehall Harbor marker.

Skenesborough Museum – The museum contains a model of Whitehall during the Revolutionary War

Whitehall

Whitehall was settled in 1759 at the southern end of Lake Champlain. Founded as the colonial town of Skenesborough by British Army Captain Philip Skene, this community became the first permanent settlement on Lake Champlain. An important center of maritime trade, Skene developed lake travel north to reach the West Indies via Quebec.

On May 9, 1775, Skenesborough was captured by American forces in the first aggressive revolutionary war action in New York State. Skene's trading schooner became the first ship of the US Navy when it was taken to Crown Point armed and used under the leadership of Col. Benedict Arnold to capture a British ship renamed Enterprise on May 18, 1775.

In 1776, Congress ordered General Philip Schuyler to construct a fleet of ships capable of countering an expected British invasion. This first US Naval fleet of thirteen ships added to the four already patrolling Lake Champlain was constructed during the summer of 1776. Led by Benedict Arnold, the action of this fleet at the battle of Vancour in October of that year caused a delaying action that ultimately saved the American Forces at Saratoga. This naval fleet was the only one to see active service in the Revolutionary War.

(Whitehall Marker)

Period and includes audio effects. The model shows a town centered around shipbuilding and a harbor full of ships.

Skene's Mills – The Lock 12 Marina is where the sawmills were located. The marina can be found by crossing the bridge over the canal and turning left onto North Williams Street. It is a few blocks up William Street. The Skene's Mill marker is between the marina and the canal and can only be seen by parking at the marina.

Skene's Mills

In this vicinity at Wood Creek Falls stood the Skenesborough mill that was used to saw plank for Benedict Arnold's 1776 Valcour fleet.

(Whitehall Marker)

Naval Artillery – The armory is the location of some of Benedict Arnold's naval artillery. The armory can be found by reversing direction on North Williams Street and following it to the intersection with

Early British Cannon

The early British Cannon placed here are from Benedict Arnold's Champlain Fleet. Both were blown up in Whitehall harbor by their crews, July 6, 1777 to avoid capture by the British.

(Whitehall Marker)

US Route 4. The armory is a very imposing castle-like structure across the street. It is the current home of Company I, 2nd Regiment, National Guard of New York. Inside the armory fence you will see two old cannons retrieved from the bottom of Lake Champlain and a marker.

British 6 Pounder

Circa 1750, Artifacts of American Lake Champlain fleet, 1776-1777. Salvaged from Whitehall harbor near Lock Site 12, 1910.

(Whitehall Marker)

WHITEHALL TO FORT ANN

Mile Mark 75.4 – From the Armory, turn left onto US Route 4 heading west and cross the bridge over the Champlain Canal. After the bridge turn left and head south on US Route 4. Watch on the left for the Burgoyne marker and a Welcome-to-Whitehall billboard behind it.

Mile Mark 76.4 – As one leaves Whitehall, one can't help but wonder why the Birthplace of the US Navy has no US Navy presence. Although recent local efforts have greatly improved the town, one wonders why today's US Navy isn't helping. Why haven't Navy veteran organizations given more of their resources to the town and its museum? Why hasn't the US Navy done the same? Is it because their true founder, Benedict Arnold, turned traitor? Do they only consider Annapolis, MD their home? – So many questions to ponder as you travel south from Whitehall on US Route 4.

Mile Mark 78.5 – Watch for a dirt road on the left that is marked as the old state road. This single lane road

---

The British under General Burgoyne

traveled south toward Fort Edward along this route in July, 1777.

(Whitehall Marker)

with grass growing in the middle is a little closer to what the road was like in 1777.

Mile Mark 82.4 – Reach the intersection where Route 22 and Route 4 divide. Continue through the intersection going south on US Route 4.

Battle Hill

At this pass was fought the Battle of Fort Ann, July 8, 1777. Here Burgoyne was first checked in his victorious march by a fierce all day battle with the Americans, which de-layed the British and made possible their de-feat at Saratoga.

This tablet is erected by the State of New York and the Town of Fort Ann, 1927.

(Fort Ann Marker)

Mile Mark 85.4 – As you approach Fort Ann, US Route 4 and the Champlain Canal squeeze between two mountains. These mountains were used to strategic advantage by American forces as the British marched south from Skenesborough.

Watch for a rocky cut taken from the mountain on the right. There is a battle marker in the middle, but it is very difficult to see – especially at 55 mph.

Mile Mark 86.0 – Cross Halfway Creek. There is a creek marker near the bridge.

Mile Mark 86.1 – Arrive in Fort Ann.

Halfway Creek

Halfway Creek was used in the French and Indian War and the Revolutionary War for transport of supplies.

(Fort Ann Marker)

FORT ANN

When you arrive in Fort Ann, you'll see a blockhouse on the left that is actually a commercial bank.

Just past the blockhouse, on the right, is a street with a "gateway to the north" marker and an "old well" marker near the Patriot Restaurant. You should turn onto this street, as US Route 4 is a very busy road through Fort Ann.

Fort Ann is still a gateway to the north. Vermont is served by interstates from the south and east, but not the west. Consequently, Fort Ann is on a major truck route between Vermont and Interstates 87 and 90 to the west.

Not far from the gateway marker is a marker for the old well that was once part of the fort at Fort Ann. The well can be seen between the restaurant and the fire station.

When advance units of the British forces began moving south in 1777, they encountered significant resistance from about 550 Americans at Fort Ann on July 8th. Although no attempt was actually made to permanently hold the position, there was a two-hour skirmish fought

---

Fort Ann

Fort Ann is the gateway to the north. Here stood five forts, 1690-1777 on the route between Lake Champlain and the Hudson River.

(Fort Ann Marker)

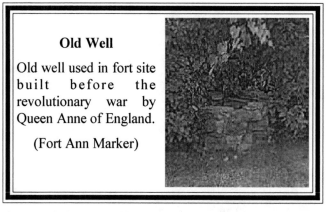

Old Well

Old well used in fort site built before the revolutionary war by Queen Anne of England.

(Fort Ann Marker)

here until it was believed that the advance units were being reinforced. During the skirmish, the British recorded the capture of an American flag with thirteen red and white stripes and a constellation. It is likely that this was the first time the stars and stripes flew in battle.

After going past the old well and turning left on Catherine Street, you can return back to US Route 4 by turning left at the busy intersection with Route 149 and right at the light. Just past the light on the left is the local library, also a great source for Fort Ann history.

As you depart Fort Ann, there's another question to ponder. Why are there no markers in Fort Ann about the flag?

Re-enactors portray Burgoyne's invasion of Fort Ann at the Fort Ann Library

FORT ANN TO OLD FORT EDWARD

Mile Mark 86.5 – Depart Fort Ann.

As you continue down US Route 4, try not to be too distracted by the farm you will pass on the south side of town. Your nose will likely cause the distraction as you pick up that natural fertilizer smell.

Mile Mark 90.8 – Watch for the marker in the center of the picturesque town of Kingsbury.

Mile Mark 94.4 – You will reach the junction with Burgoyne Avenue that is

Burgoyne's army marched over this trail, July 29, 1777 to defeat at Saratoga on October 17, 1777.

(Kingsbury Marker)

74

Kingsbury Street

The first settler of this neighborhood was Oliver Colvin, who came here in 1766, and was the second pioneer of the Town of Kingsbury. At one time there were two churches, a school, post office, several taverns, hotels, stores, and mills located in this hamlet.

Erected by the Town of Kingsbury, 1999, with New York State funds.

(Kingsbury Marker)

---

also Route 32. Route 32 parallels parts of US Route 4 and will reappear several times along the way to Albany.

This part of US Route 4 was a carrying route (portage) between Lake Champlain and the Hudson River. Glens Falls, which is about 3 miles to the west, was also part of a carrying route between Lake Champlain and the Hudson River. The Glens Falls route used the entire length of Lake George.

In 1777, Burgoyne used both of these routes. After pursuing the American forces to Skeenesborough, the Fort Ann route was the shortest distance for the British to get to the Hudson River. Since most of their artillery and supplies were still back at Fort Ticonderoga, Burgoyne sent them by way of Glens Falls. Some believe that he did this because he knew the Americans were somewhere to his east and, this way, he could better protect his supply line. Although this route was the shortest route for the British troops, Americans did much to slow their progress by felling trees and destroying bridges.

Mile Mark 95.4 – Cross a small bridge over a feeder canal that connects to the Champlain Canal. The canal solves a problem the Champlain canal has at this point. The canal has reached a high point. Lake Champlain is at a lower elevation to the north and the Hudson River is at a lower elevation to the south. Consequently, the feeder canal supplies water from  the upper Hudson River to the canal at this elevation.

Mile Mark 95.7 – You will soon reach Hudson Falls. Watch for the library on the left. There is a Knox Trail

This memorial cannon is dedicated to the soldiers who fought and died in the area during the Revolutionary War. Dedicated on July 4, 1976.

(Hudson Falls Marker)

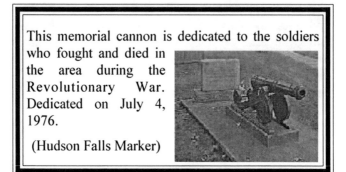

marker in front of the library.

In the center of town there is a rotary with a monument to LaFayette who stayed at Judge Baker's home during a visit to the town in 1825. The rotary surrounds a park, which contains a small cannon and a Washington marker.

Mile Mark 96.3 – Watch for a LaFayette marker just south of the rotary on the right. It stands to the left between a used car lot and the Judge Baker home.

As you continue your travel through the town, you can sense the Hudson River close by, since there is a

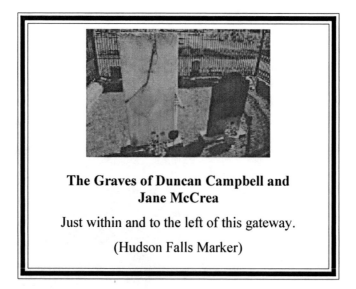

The Graves of Duncan Campbell and Jane McCrea

Just within and to the left of this gateway.

(Hudson Falls Marker)

considerable drop-off on the right side of the road. But, unfortunately, buildings prevent any view of the river. It's a little paradoxical that you can't see the Hudson fall through Hudson Falls.

Mile Mark 96.9 – Watch for a marker in front of a cemetery on the left where Duncan Campbell and Jane McCrea are buried. Campbell died of wounds he received on July 17, 1758 at Fort Ticonderoga during the French and Indian War. Jane McCrea's grave marker is hard to read but most of the words can be deciphered.

Probably, the worst fear of any military officer is the accidental killing of innocent civilians that inevitably get caught in the middle of battle. Burgoyne employed Native American Indians in his army, primarily in

78

> Here rests the remains of Jane McCrea, aged 17, made captive and murdered by a band of Indians, while on a visit to a relative in this neighborhood, AD 1777.
>
> To commemorate one of the most thrilling incidents in the annals of the American Revolution to do justice to the fame of the . . . British Officer to whom she was . . . and as simple tribute to the memory of the departed, this stone was erected by her niece, Sara Hanna Payne, A.D. 1852.
>
> (Cemetery Grave Marker)

scouting missions ahead of his main army. The problem was their custom of taking scalps, something that Burgoyne seemed to reluctantly accept in return for their loyalty and cooperation.

Jane McCrea, a young, beautiful girl with long black hair was betrothed to one of Burgoyne's officers. Tragically, she became a civilian caught in the middle of a skirmish between Indians near Fort Edward. She was killed and her scalp was taken. The scalp was recognized immediately by the anguished officer and he demanded that Burgoyne punish the Indian by death. Out of fear of causing a mass desertion of all the

> ### Jane McCrea
>
> Killed on 27 July 1777, a short distance to the south of this spot. Her death helped to defeat General Burgoyne at Saratoga.
>
> 2001 by WCHS & T. Fort Edward
>
> (Fort Edward Marker)

Indians, Burgoyne left the punishment to the Indian chief, which meant practically no punishment at all.

The story of Jane McCrea traveled quickly. It soon became a rallying cry for Americans and helped to swell the ranks forming for the Battles of Saratoga. In England, it fed the fire of those who were against the war and contributed greatly to its growing unpopularity.

Mile Mark 97.8 – Watch for another Knox Trail marker on the left in front of Fort Edward High School.

Across the street is a monument to Jane McCrea.

> Old Military Road went diagonally up this hill 1758-1777.
>
> (Fort Edward Marker)

The monument is hard to see because it is between two homes and is protected by a fence. The monument marks the place where Jane McCrea was killed.

Just past the high school on the left, as you come down a hill into Fort Edward, is a military road marker. This part of US Route 4 is the old military road between Albany and Whitehall.

Mile Mark 98.5 – Watch for the Jane McCrea house on the right.

Mile Mark 98.8 – Arrive at Old Fort Edward.

81

OLD FORT EDWARD

Just past the intersection with Route 197 is the Anvil Restaurant and Lounge. There are two markers near the restaurant. The first marker is out near Route 4. It indicates that this was the site of the North East Bastion of Old Fort Edward. The second marker, "The Great Carrying Place," is actually inside the restaurant's fenced in area for outdoor eating.

You can reach additional markers by detouring off US Route 4 straight past the Anvil Restaurant toward the Hudson River and turning right on Old Fort Street. On the right, in the middle of a side yard of a neighborhood home is a moat marker. This little neighborhood happens to be in the middle of what used to be a big old fort.

Remains of Old Moat

Part of the outworks of Fort Edward

(Fort Edward Marker)

A little further down the street is a dead end. You should see a very small park at the end of the street, but be warned, the property to the left of the park is posted. The owner often parks his truck in front of the park.

If you can find a place to park, there is a little park that overlooks a bend in the Hudson River. It is easy to see

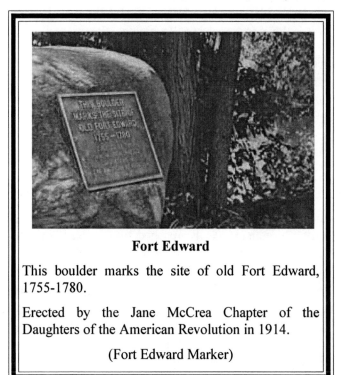

Fort Edward

This boulder marks the site of old Fort Edward, 1755-1780.

Erected by the Jane McCrea Chapter of the Daughters of the American Revolution in 1914.

(Fort Edward Marker)

The Smythe House

Erected by Patrick Smythe about 1767 of timber taken from Fort Edward. The first tavern and scene of the first court in Charlotte County. Headquarters of Schuyler, Arnold, Burgoyne, and Stark in 1777. It is the oldest house in Washington County.

(Smythe House Marker)

why a fort at this strategic position would easily control access to the Hudson River and thereby control the two routes to Lake Champlain. In the park is a boulder with a marker on it.

Since this is not a very wide road, turning around is a bit tricky. You might want to back down street.

Just south of Old Fort Edward is the Old Fort House Gift Museum. It can be reached by returning back to US Route 4 and going south around a couple bends. There are several markers at the house.

Old Fort Edward is actually a part of the house. As the stone marker explains, timber taken from the fort was used for building in 1767. Because this was done, the old fort was in no condition for battle when Philip Schuyler inspected it in 1777. Consequently, the

General Washington

In the summer of 1783, General George Washington was a guest here at Sherwood's House or Tavern while on a tour of the area battlefields.

(Smythe House Marker)

Americans had to find a place further south for their stand against the British. If the fort was in better condition, the Americans could have used the fort as a base of operations to split the British forces from their supplies.

Near Here Stood the Red House

Mentioned in Madame Riedesel's memoirs built about 1766.

(Smythe House Marker)

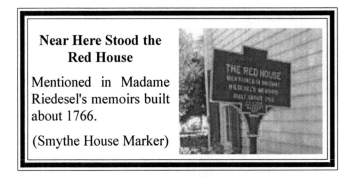

FORT EDWARD TO FORT MILLER

Mile Mark 99.3 – As you depart Fort Edward and cross the Champlain Canal, watch for Lock 7 on the right. This lock connects the canal with the Hudson River. From this point on, the canal shares the same route as the Hudson River to reach Albany.

Mile Mark 101.5 – Watch on the right for what looks like a grave stone and a Jane McCrea marker.

The Original Burial Place of Jane McCrea

July 28, 1777. Near this spot lies the body of Tobias Van Veghten, a lieutenant in Colonel McCrea's regiment killed at the Jane McCrea massacre, July 27, 1777.

(Fort Miller Marker)

Based on the marker, we conclude that Jane McCrea's remains were moved from this location to the cemetery near Hudson Falls. We also see the power of words. The "tragic, accidental death of Jane McCrea" does not nearly have as much impact as the "Jane McCrea Massacre." The latter stirs the emotions and becomes a rallying cry.

Mile Mark 104.6 – The Champlain Canal reappears on the right side of the road as you approach the town of Fort Miller. Fort Miller is one of the places along the Hudson where boats had to be taken out of the river due to natural waterfalls and shallow rapids. Today, these areas have been tamed by dams, locks and canals that skirt around these problem areas. As a result, the town of Fort Miller is now on an island with the Hudson River on the west and the Champlain Canal on the east.

Mile Mark 106.2 – Watch for the Fort Miller marker on the right just past the second bridge across the canal. The original Fort Miller was on the west side of the Hudson River.

On the opposite side of the river, Fort Miller, built during the French and Indian War.

(Fort Miller Marker)

Duer House

British Headquarters, August 14-September 10, 1777.

(Fort Miller Marker)

Mile Mark 106.4 – On the left side of the road, there is a marker for the Duer House. About a quarter mile up the road, there is a house marker on the left.

Mile Mark 107.5 – Detour right at this entrance to Fort Miller. In the middle of the intersection on a grassy island, there is another Knox Trail marker. Cross the bridge over the Champlain canal and loop through the town of Fort Miller.

Arrive in Fort Miller.

FORT MILLER

Fort Miller is a pretty little village on the Hudson River. There are no stores and just one church on this side of the canal. Overlooking the river, there are many quaint and beautiful homes.

Where Fort Edward was a carrying place, this area was a gathering place.

A July 1777 Gathering Place – About 2,500 retreating Americans gathered here about a week after a long circuitous retreat that began on July 5th:

- Started at Fort Ticonderoga after the British began moving artillery up Mount Defiance.

- Crossed Lake Champlain to Vermont on the floating bridge.

- Through Mount Independence picking up the Americans stationed there.

- Down the old military road through Hubbardton where a pursuing British detachment would be halted.

- Through Castleton then east to Rutland so they would avoid meeting the British at Skenesborough.

- Marched south to Manchester.

- Trekked southwest along the Battenkill River from Manchester to Fort Miller completing a journey that totaled about 100 miles.

They arrived at Fort Miller hungry, exhausted, poorly clothed and totally disorganized. Under the leadership of General Philip Schuyler, they recovered, regrouped, reorganized and began preparation to meet the British forces moving south from Skenesborough.

An August 1777 Gathering Place – Burgoyne arrived with British forces numbering close to 8,000. He found no resistance here, since the Americans had moved to positions further south. Shortly after their arrival, Burgoyne launched an expedition of about 1,000 troops to the east toward Bennington to obtain horses and supplies. Most of the troops that Burgoyne sent would not return as the Americans won a decisive victory near Bennington and imprisoned those that surrendered.

Despite the loss, Burgoyne was determined to carry out his mission and continue his drive for the conquest of Albany. His problem was the Hudson River. Albany is on the west side of the Hudson and he and his forces were on the east side. Furthermore, once they crossed the Hudson, the river would sever their supply line. Therefore, Burgoyne had to build up enough supplies to complete his mission before crossing the Hudson. That turned out to be a real problem, because his supply line now stretched all the way back to Canada. At best, the supply line would bring down four day's rations, but often it would not even provide a day's worth.

Finally, on September 13th, almost a month after they had arrived, the British crossed the Hudson River and headed south toward Albany.

FORT MILLER TO SCHUYLERVILLE

Mile Mark 108.1 – After looping through Fort Miller and recrossing the Champlain Canal, turn right and continue south on US Route 4. With all the gathering that occurred here, it's a wonder why there are no historical markers in the town.

Mile Mark 109.7 – Watch for a surviving portion of the old Champlain Canal on the left. Near the canal is a marker for Washington's visit to Greenwich, NY in 1783.

Mile Mark 111.1 – You will reach a narrow bridge that crosses the Hudson River. If there is any traffic coming across, it's probably a good idea to wait before crossing.

Just after the bridge, you will reach a stop sign at an intersection with Route 32. Turn left and continue south on US 4.

You are now on the west bank of the Hudson River, just as the British were in September of 1777. The British traveled this route in three columns with flags flying, drums drumming and bands playing. What an incongruous sight this must have been along this old

General Washington

In the summer of 1783, General George Washington was in the township of Greenwich, while on a tour of northern battlefields.

By W.C.H.S. 1999

(Greenwich Marker)

military road in the wilderness along the Hudson River.

Mile Mark 111.7 – On the right side of the road near a home there is a Stark marker. This marker indicates that after the British had passed through this area, American troops moved in behind the British to surround them. In

Schuylerville, you will see a Daniel Morgan marker for an American position that prevented British retreat to the west. Just past the marker on the right is an intersection at which there are several flags as well as a Knox Trail marker. Stark's Knob is a short distance up the street and parking can be found at the base of this old volcanic knob. However, it is not recommended that you try to climb the rocky knob from the parking

Stark's Knob and the American Revolution

Near the end of the "Battles of Saratoga," General John Stark and his American troops fortified a low hill in the gap between Stark's Knob and the Hudson River wetlands. The British army had retreated from American troops further south, and was camped and fully under siege on October 13, 1777, on the heights now occupied by the Village of Schuylerville. Stark's action blocked the escape route of the British army and its German troops north to Ticonderoga and Canada. The blocking of the road in the gap between Stark's emplacement and the hill now known as Stark's Knob completed, as historian John Brandow has described it, "the corking of the bottle."

No evidence for the popular belief that General Stark placed artillery on Stark's Knob to stop the British can be found in the historical record. However, the strategic location of Stark's Knob contributed to the surrender of the British army on October 17, 1777 — the "Turning Point of the American Revolution."

(Schuylerville Marker)

lot. There is a path just up the street across from a nearby home. At the top of the knob is a marker as well is a very scenic view of the Hudson.

Mile Mark 112.7 – Reach the village of Schuylerville.

Surrender of General Burgoyne
by John Trumbull

SCHUYLERVILLE

In the months prior to October 8, 1777, the British suffered about 2,000 casualties. Burgoyne's forces, now down to about 6,000 men, took refuge in a fortified camp on the heights of Saratoga (today's Schuylerville). There an American force that was approaching 20,000 men surrounded the exhausted British army.

Faced with such overwhelming numbers, Burgoyne surrendered on October 17, 1777. By the terms of the

Convention of Saratoga, Burgoyne's depleted army marched out of camp "with the Honors of War" and stacked their weapons along the west bank of the Hudson River at Fort Hardy.

Saratoga Monument

The Saratoga Monument commemorates the surrender of the British Army under the command of General John Burgoyne to General Horatio Gates commander of the America forces on 17 October 1777 following the battles of Saratoga. The battles and subsequent surrender are considered a turning point in the American Revolution by leading to French support and the hope of ultimate victory. This lofty sight was chosen for the monument because of its commanding view of the surrounding battlefield sites and its historical association with Burgoyne's campaign. The cornerstone was laid on 17 October 1877, one hundred years after the British surrender. The capstone was put into place in 1882 and the decorative elements of bronze statues and interior bass relief was finally completed in 1887. A cast iron stairway lead up 184 steps to an observation deck which is closed.

(Schuylerville Marker)

Saratoga was a decisive and important victory. It was the turning point of the American Revolution.

Saratoga Monument – To see the many historical sites around Schuylerville, a loop around town similar to the one taken in Fort Miller is recommended. The first site can be reached by going through most of the downtown area and turning right at Burgoyne Avenue, also County Route 338. Just up the street is the Saratoga Monument.

The monument commemorates the surrender of British Forces to

Saratoga Monument

The three statues on the outside niches are bronze presentations of the major American players in the Battles of Saratoga. General Philip Schuyler, commander of the American forces during the greater part of the British invasion faces east toward his home. General Horatio Gates faces north. General Daniel Morgan, commander of the riflemen, faces west. The vacant niche facing south is in recognition of the leadership of Benedict Arnold who in 1780 turned traitor to the American cause.

(Schuylerville Marker)

American Forces on October 17, 1777. As explained by the marker in front of the monument, each side of the monument has a niche for each of the major American contributors in the Battles of Saratoga: Philip Schuyler, Daniel Morgan, Horatio Gates and Benedict Arnold.

The monument was refurbished in 2002 for the 225th Anniversary of the British surrender. Before refurbishing, one could not help but notice a little tree growing in the vacant niche where the statue of Benedict Arnold would have been. One wondered if Arnold was building his own statue from the grave.

A climb to the top of the monument is recommended for the non-acrophobic.

Colonel Morgan

Colonel Morgan held this position to prevent British retreat to the west.

(Schuylerville Marker)

Campground of the British Army

October 15, 1777.

(Schuylerville Marker)

Revolutionary War Markers on the North Side of Schuylerville – Continuing past the Saratoga Monument and bearing right at the next several intersections, you will pass an old graveyard and several markers.

The first marker is at the position that Daniel Morgan and his riflemen took to stop a possible British retreat to the west. The marker is near a small cemetery where many of the graves date back to the middle 1800's. Just past the cemetery at an intersection with Route 29 is a marker about the town of Saratoga.

A series of four markers can be found aloung Route 29 on the return back US Route 4. There are two British

Town of Saratoga

Mother town of Saratoga County. First European settlers, 1688. Established, March 7, 1788. Surrender sight of General Burgoyne to General Gates, October 17, 1777.

(Schuylerville Marker)

Continental Barracks

Where General Stark tried and condemned the Tory, Lovelass as a spy.

Camp of General Burgoyne
October 10-17, 1777.

(Schuylerville Marker)

---

encampment markers on the left. One is near a gift shop. The other is in front of a home near the Schuylerville Central School. There is a breastworks marker on the right opposite the school and there is a barracks marker on the left, just before the intersection with US Route 4.

Fort Hardy Park – Returning to US Route 4 south and turning left onto Broadway, you will cross the old Champlain Canal and Tow Path and eventually come to Fort Hardy Park.

On these fields, the British Army grounded arms at the surrender.

(Schuylerville Marker)

The park is site where the British laid down their arms after the battles of Saratoga. Today, Fort Hardy is an athletic park with soccer fields and other athletic facilities. Keeping the history alive on the west side of the field is the Schuylerville Visitor Center. Inside, there are history exhibits as well as information about Schuylerville. Near the Visitor Center is a marker for the Surrender Tree, under which the surrender

The Surrender Tree

The tree commemorates a great elm tree, under which it is said, the British General John Burgoyne signed the Convention of Saratoga by which he surrendered his forces to American General Horatio Gates, October 17, 1777. Considered to be the turning point of the American Revolution.

(Schuylerville Marker)

Near this spot, October 16, 1777, American and British officers met and consummated "Articles of Convention" of General Burgoyne of the British army to General Gates of the American army and on this historic ground of Saratoga the British army laid down its arms, October 17, 1777 thus assuring American independence.

(Schuylerville Marker)

documents were signed. There is also a surrender marker near the entrance to the park.

Revolutionary War Markers in Schuylerville – Returning back to US Route 4 and going through downtown once again, there is a Conventions of Saratoga marker on the left near the center of town.

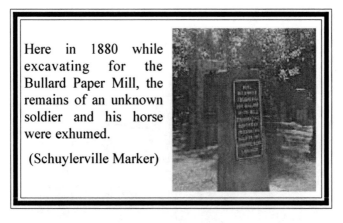

Here in 1880 while excavating for the Bullard Paper Mill, the remains of an unknown soldier and his horse were exhumed.

(Schuylerville Marker)

There are also two markers on the left just before the bridge across the Fishkill River. One of the two is a Knox Trail marker. The other is about the recovery of a soldier and a horse.

Schuyler House – Just across the Fishkill River bridge on the left is the Schuyler House. Across from the house on the west side of Route 4 is a Schuyler family marker. The marker shows the sacrifice made by the Schuyler family to colonize this area.

November 28, 1745, on these grounds the French and Indians killed Captain Philip Schuyler and thirty others, burning mills, stores and thirty houses.

On June 30, 1747, the garrison of Fort Saratoga was surprised when 45 men were tomahawked and scalped.

Site of the house of Captain Schuyler, 1745 and General Philip Schuyler, 1777.

(Schuylerville Marker)

Schuyler House

"We passed Hudson's River and encamped in the plains of Saratoga at which place there is a handsome and commodious dwelling house," so wrote an officer of British General John Burgoyne's invading army in September 1777. The dwelling house was the country home of wealthy landowner, Philip Schuyler. Less than a month later, his army reeling in defeat, Burgoyne ordered the house burned so the Americans could not use it for cover. Despite this precaution, the proud Burgoyne was forced to surrender his army on October 17, 1777 in a field not far from the smoldering ruins. Within weeks, Schuyler was earnestly engaged in building a house at this place. By the end of November 1777, the present building was completed, possibly built in part on the foundation of the old dwelling house. The present Schuyler House has been carefully restored to its 1787-1804 appearance.

(Schuylerville Marker)

In front of the Schuyler house, there is a marker at the pathway entrance that relates its history. Depending on the time of the year, volunteers in period costume may be on hand to give you a tour of the house. Tours are scheduled on the half-hour.

SCHUYLERVILLE TO THE
SARATOGA BATTLEFIELD

Mile Mark 117.0 – Depart the country home of Philip Schuyler. Schuyler's winter home is in Albany, the last stop on this **Revolutionary Day**.

Mile Mark 117.7 – Watch for the intersection with Schuyler Street. Note the name on the mailbox across the street.

This little corner is very historical. On the right, up the hill, just to the left of the street is a surrender marker.

Mile Mark 118.2 – In front of two homes on the left, there is a Gates Headquarters marker. If you pull over

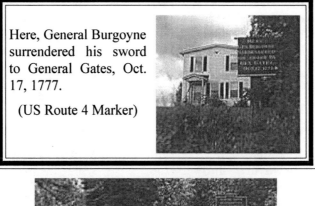

Here, General Burgoyne surrendered his sword to General Gates, Oct. 17, 1777.

(US Route 4 Marker)

for a closer look at the marker, watch out for the dogs.

Mile Mark 119.4 – In front of a farm on the left is a Dovegat House marker.

Mile Mark 121.8 – There are nice views of the Hudson River on the left.

Mile Mark 123.4 – Enter National Park Lands. The Saratoga Battlefield National Park encompasses several square miles. You are now driving through the location of the British Hospital during the Battles of Saratoga.

Dovegat House

Headquarters, General Burgoyne during the advance and retreat of the British Army.

(US Route 4 Marker)

The Great Redoubt
by Barlow

Keep an eye to the right and you will see several high hills. These hills are part of a redoubt, a British defensive position. Although you can't see them, there are British cannons targeting the very area you are now passing through.

Mile Mark 123.8 – Turn right and enter the Saratoga Battlefield National Park.

107

SARATOGA BATTLEFIELD

The Visitor Center for the Saratoga Battlefield National Park is about two miles from the entrance on US Route 4.

The road around the battlefield is a one-way toll road and you need to go to the Visitor Center for the $5 pass to use the road. Also in the Visitor Center is a museum, a gift shop and a theatre. The theatre plays a film that

To the Left — Breymann Redoubt — .5 Miles

Straight Ahead — Balcarres Redoubt — .75 Miles

To the Right — American Camp — 2 Miles

(Saratoga Marker)

200th Anniversary, 1777-1977
Battles of Saratoga

These fields now echo the sounds of silence and peace thanks to the men who won American victory.

Placed by the Admiral George Brown Chapter of the Empire State Society Sons of the American Revolution.

(Saratoga Battlefield)

---

introduces visitors to the Battles of Saratoga.

With the toll road pass, you will receive a pamphlet that can be used in conjunction with the maps and exhibits in  the Visitor Center and the interpretive markers on the battlefield itself to help you understand the Battles of Saratoga. The complete tour, which begins at the south end of the parking area, covers over 9 miles and contains 10 tour stops. Although the tour is set up primarily for automobiles, bicycles are also very popular. In addition, there are walking paths and trails for horses.

In the back of the Visitor Center is a directional sign marker and a 200th Anniversary marker.

THE BATTLE AT FREEMAN'S FARM
SEPTEMBER 19, 1777

The First Battle of Saratoga – On the 19th of September 1777, British Forces under the command of General Burgoyne advanced south in three separate columns upon the American Forces who had set up defenses here. Two of the columns moved through the forests covering the region just west of the Hudson River. The third, composed of German troops, marched down the old military road along the river.

American scouts first detected Burgoyne's forces and notified General Gates, who ordered Colonel Daniel Morgan's Virginia riflemen to track the British advance. Shortly after 12 PM, some of Morgan's men made contact with the advance guard of the center column. The contact took place in a clearing known as the Freeman Farm, which is Tour Stop 1.

Tour Stop 1 – Freeman Farm. The battle that followed swayed back and forth over the farm for more than three hours. However, in the face of deadly fire from the numerically superior Americans, the British lines began to waver. But then German reinforcements arrived from the military road and attacked the American right, Burgoyne was able to steady the British lines and gradually force the Americans to withdraw back to the American camp near Neilson Farm, which is Tour Stop 2.

Just before the stop is a monument placed in memory of Thaddeus

Kosciuszko. Thousands of commuters are very familiar with another tribute to this great war hero – The Thaddeus Kosciuszko Bridge across the Mohawk River on the Northway (Interstate 87).

Across from the Kosciuszko monument is an area set aside for the unknown soldiers of Saratoga. A memorial is located near several unmarked graves.

Tour Stop 2 – Neilson Farm. American staff officers used Neilson Farm for quarters. Near the farm is a line of white polls that mark American positions. Down the hill there is a line of blue

Thaddeus Kosciuszko
by H. B. Hall

polls that mark British positions.

On the 19th of September 1777, the timely arrival of the German troops and the near exhaustion of the American's ammunition allowed Burgoyne to reach these positions. The British commander ordered his troops to entrench in the vicinity of the Freeman Farm and await support from British Forces under the command of General Clinton, who was supposedly preparing to move north toward Albany from New York City. For nearly three weeks he waited, but Clinton did not arrive.

Though he held the immediate field of battle, Burgoyne had been stopped north of the American line that stretched from Bemis Heights to the powerful river fortifications near the Hudson River, which is Tour Stop 3.

American River Fortifications

This powerful position was established under the direction of Col. Thaddeus Kosciuszko, a Polish military engineer and volunteer in the patriot cause, and it proved to be the key to American strategy against Burgoyne in 1777. Patriot infantry and cannon posted here, supported by batteries along the near riverbank, closed off the Hudson Valley route to Albany and forced the British to attack the main American line on Bemis Heights on September 19.

(Saratoga Marker)

Tour Stop 3 – River Fortifications. At this position, you can hear the traffic going by on US Route 4 below. You cannot see the road, but in 1777 the trees would have been cleared.

Anchor of the American Line

Artillery and Infantry positions along this bluff commanded the road to Albany. This defense line forced the British to fight on American terms.

(Saratoga Marker)

If the Redcoats had advanced down the road below toward Albany, the guns of this strongpoint would have been the first to greet them. In 1777, the road swung from its present route diagonally across the field below you toward the river.

(Saratoga Marker)

The Second Battle of Saratoga – By the 7th of October 1777, Burgoyne's situation was critical. Faced by a growing American army and no help from Clinton from the south, and supplies

Chatfield Farm

An American outpost on this ridge, the site of Asa Chatfield's farm in 1777, spotted the British movement toward the Barber Farm on October 7. Beyond the ridge before you is Middle Ravine, across which American and British pickets exchanged musket shots between the first and second battles.

(Saratoga Exhibit & Marker)

rapidly diminishing, the British army was becoming weaker with each passing day. Burgoyne had to choose between advancing or retreating. He ordered a reconnaissance-in-force to test the American left flank. Ably led and supported by eight cannon, a force of 1,500 men moved out of the British camp. An American outpost on a ridge near Chatfield Farm, which is Tour Stop 4, spotted the British movement.

Tour Stop 4 – Chatfield Farm. After marching southwesterly about three quarters of a mile, the troops deployed in a clearing on the Barber Farm, which is

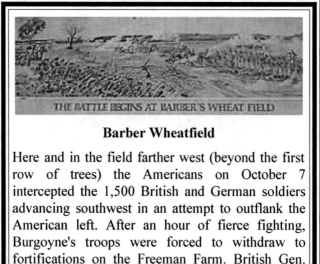

THE BATTLE BEGINS AT BARBER'S WHEAT FIELD

Barber Wheatfield

Here and in the field farther west (beyond the first row of trees) the Americans on October 7 intercepted the 1,500 British and German soldiers advancing southwest in an attempt to outflank the American left. After an hour of fierce fighting, Burgoyne's troops were forced to withdraw to fortifications on the Freeman Farm. British Gen. Simon Fraser was mortally wounded northwest of here while trying to rally his men.

(Saratoga Marker)

Tour Stop 5. Most of the British were positioned in an open field, but both flanks rested in woods.

Tour Stop 5 – Barber Farm. The Americans knew that Burgoyne's army was again on the move and at about 3 PM attacked in three columns under Colonel Morgan, General Ebenezer Learned, and General

Re-enactors Move into Position at Saratoga

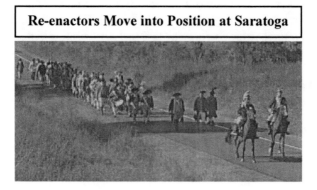

Enoch Poor. Repeatedly, the British line was broken, then rallied. Both flanks were severely punished and driven back. General Simon Fraser, who commanded the British right, was mortally wounded as he rode among his men encouraging them to stand and cover the developing withdrawal.

Before the enemy's flanks could be rallied, General Benedict Arnold, who had been relieved of command after a quarrel with Gates, rode onto the field and led Learned's brigade against the German troops holding the British center. Under tremendous pressure from all sides, the Germans joined a general withdrawal into the fortifications on the Freeman Farm. Within an hour

Balcarres Redoubt

(Freeman Farm)

Balcarres Redoubt was a log-and-earthen work about 500 yards long and 12 to 14 feet high. Named for Lord Balcarres, who commanded the British light infantry, it formed the strongest part of the fortified line constructed between the Hudson River and the Breymann Redoubt by Burgoyne's troops after the battle of September 19. On October 7 the British flanking column withdrew here after being driven from the Barber Farm. The redoubt is outlined by posts.

(Saratoga Exhibit & Marker)

after the opening clash, Burgoyne lost eight cannon and more than 400 officers and men.

Flushed with success, the Americans believed that victory was near. Arnold led one column in a series of savage attacks on the Balcarres Redoubt, which is Tour Stop 6. The redoubt was a powerful British fieldwork on the Freeman Farm.

While Morgan's Light Corps, the 5th and 6th Massachusetts Continentals and other American troops, attacked the Breymann Redoubt from the front, the intrepid Benedict Arnold without a command of his own joined a handful of Americans on a daring assault from the rear. Near this spot, Arnold was shot in the leg. The nameless boot monument symbolizes his bravery as well as his subsequent treason.

(Saratoga Marker)

Tour Stop 6 – Balcarres Redoubt. After repeated American failures to carry Balcarres Redoubt, General Benedict Arnold wheeled his horse and dashed through the crossfire of both armies to the Breymann Redoubt, which is Tour Stop 7. Arnold arrived just as American troops began their assault on British fortifications. He joined in the final surge that overwhelmed the German soldiers defending the work. Upon entering the

Breymann Redoubt

Breymann Redoubt, also outlined by posts, was a single line of breastworks about 200 yards long and 7 to 8 feet high. It guarded the British right flank and the road to Quaker Springs. It was named for Lt. Col. Heinrich Breymann, whose German troops were stationed here.

(Saratoga Marker)

redoubt, he was wounded in the leg. Had he died during this assault, there is no doubt that posterity would have known few names more heroic than that of General Benedict Arnold.

Failing to capture Balcarres Redoubt, the Americans surged against Crown Forces fortifications built here called the Breymann Redoubt. Attacking relentlessly they overwhelmed this important defensive position just before nightfall, October 7, 1777. Never more than a crude barrier of logs, this fortification is now known as the Breymann Redoubt, named after the German officer who commanded the German Grenadier defenders.

(Saratoga Marker)

Tour Stop 7 – Breymann Redoubt. Darkness ended the day's fighting and saved Burgoyne's army from immediate defeat. That night the British commander left his campfires burning, abandoned British Headquarters, which is Tour Stop 8, and began pulling his forces back to the North.

Benedict Arnold by H. B. Hall

Tour Stop 8 – British Headquarters. Burgoyne withdrew his troops behind the Great Redoubt that protected the high ground and river flats at the northeast corner of the battlefield.

After you leave Tour Stop 8, you will cross a high bridge over a stream and the entrance road that, at this point, parallels the stream. The high ground that you are traveling to is the Great Redoubt and includes Tour Stops 9 and 10.

Burgoyne's Headquarters

The path here leads to the site of Burgoyne's headquarters, which at the time of the battles consisted of a large marquee or tent. It was established after the action of September 19 and was the center of British command and camp life between the two battles. Burgoyne chose the location because of a nearby spring.

(Saratoga Marker)

Tour Stop 9 – Great Redoubt. From the top of the redoubt, there is a view of the entrance to the park on US Route 4 and the Hudson River in the distance. Picnic tables make it a great spot for an afternoon picnic or just a

The Great Redoubt

The Great Redoubt was a system of fortifications built by the British on this hill and two others to the north. It was designed to guard their hospital, artillery park, and supplies on the river flat, and the boat bridge across the Hudson. Burgoyne withdrew his army to this vicinity during the night of October 7.

(Saratoga Marker)

> The capture of the Breymann Redoubt forced Burgoyne to withdraw his army to a position centered on three fortifications. This is the second of these three fortifications that were referred to by the British as the Great Redoubt. They were built sometime between September 19th and October 7th, 1777.
>
> (Saratoga Marker)

place to sit and contemplate the events of 1777.

On the night of the 8th of October 1777, the British buried General Fraser and began a hasty retreat northward. They had suffered about 1,000 casualties in the fighting of the past three weeks; American losses numbered less than 500. Saratoga was one of the most decisive victories in American and world history. It helped to convince the French to join

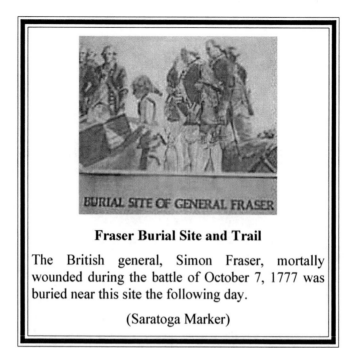

BURIAL SITE OF GENERAL FRASER

Fraser Burial Site and Trail

The British general, Simon Fraser, mortally wounded during the battle of October 7, 1777 was buried near this site the following day.

(Saratoga Marker)

the American cause, making it the turning point of the American Revolution.

Tour Stop 10 – Walking Trail. This tour stop commemorates the burial place of General Fraser and the British retreat. The tour stop is actually a walking trail that begins with a warning marker.

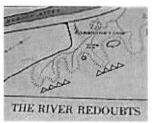

THE RIVER REDOUBTS

Beyond the gravesite, the trail goes to another site on the Great Redoubt. It continues down a steep hill between two fortifications and at the base of the hill, you reach an intersection at the base of the Great

WARNING

Steep Grade

8/10ths of a Mile in Length

No Wheelchairs

(Saratoga Marker)

Redoubt. There is no indicator which direction to go, but if you take the trail to right, you will reach a marker for the British Hospital.

Main Crown Forces Hospital

Burgoyne's retreating army was forced to leave its sick and wounded to the care of the Americans. The main British medical facilities were located on the flat below to your right.

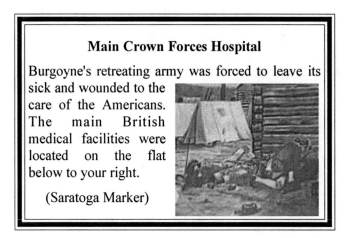

(Saratoga Marker)

Crown Forces Artillery Park

When Burgoyne ordered his army into retreat, the British force's artillery park located on the flat area below and to your right became a scene of frantic activity. The artillery equipment assembled here, larger field guns, spare carriages, carts for ammunition and tools, supply wagons, and even carriages for pontoons used to build floating bridges, all had to be hitched to oxen or horse and brought into line.

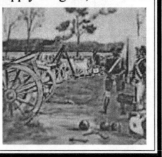

(Saratoga Marker)

Reversing direction, you will pass several markers, including a marker for the artillery park and another for the extensive baggage carried by the British forces.

Further down the trail is another intersection. Bearing to the right, you will cross a bridge that is near a

Crown Forces Baggage Park

When the order came to retreat, the civilian teamsters contracted by the British, many from Canada, began harnessing teams of horses and yoking pairs of oxen in the baggage park on the flat directly below you. Wagons and two wheeled carts, not already loaded, were hurriedly piled with officer's bedding, trunks and beds, pots and pans, barrels, and sacks of foodstuffs.

(Saratoga Marker)

SURVIVING PORTION OF CHAMPLAIN CANAL

surviving portion of the Old Champlain Canal built in the 1820's. Out, in a swampy field, one can see four posts which mark the corners of Taylor Cabin, where Simon Fraser died.

At this point, you may become aware of how deeply you have traveled into the marshy woods. Don't be surprised if you hear the sounds of creatures lurking about.

Reversing direction once again and bearing right at the

Site of the Taylor Cabin

A grievously wounded Simon Fraser was carried here to the Taylor Cabin, which had been taken over as a residence by Baroness Riedesel, the wife of the German commander. The bleeding General was brought into the room where a cheerful dinner party to which he had been invited was being held. Simon Fraser died at 8:00 on the morning of October 8, 1777.

(Saratoga Marker)

intersection, you will return back to the parking lot, but not after a healthy climb up a steep hill. There are benches on the way where you can rest during the climb.

Back in the car, the tour ends at an intersection with the entrance road. Total mileage in the park is about 12 miles.

Baroness Riedesel
by Tischbein

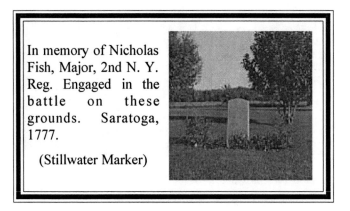

In memory of Nicholas Fish, Major, 2nd N. Y. Reg. Engaged in the battle on these grounds. Saratoga, 1777.

(Stillwater Marker)

SARATOGA BATTLEFIELD TO STILLWATER

Mile Mark 135.7 – Depart Saratoga Battlefield. As you continue south on US Route 4, you will actually cross from the southern-most, British-held territory to the northern-most American-held territory. Don't look for a marker that denotes this southern extent of the British invasion of 1777, there isn't one.

However, there is, on the left, a memorial to Major Nicholas Fish.

Mile Mark 137.4 – Saratoga Sod Farm is on the left. This area was clearly visible from the American positions up on the hill. One wonders how many people

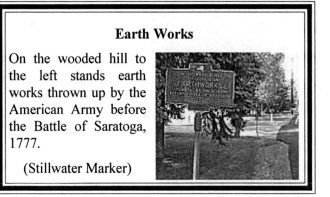

Earth Works

On the wooded hill to the left stands earth works thrown up by the American Army before the Battle of Saratoga, 1777.

(Stillwater Marker)

have driven down this part of US Route 4, not realizing that their car is targeted by cannons up on the hill.

Mile Mark 140.0 – As you get closer to the center of Stillwater, you will see an Earth Works marker on the right, in the front yard of a house. Good luck finding the earth works. Today, the area is covered by homes.

Mile Mark 140.4 – Arrive in Stillwater.

Ferry Lane

October 17, 1777, Burgoyne's Brunswick troops marched through this lane to Vandenburgh Ferry and prison camp at Cambridge, Massachusetts.

(Stillwater Marker)

STILLWATER

Ferry Lane – As you near the center of Stillwater, you will pass Ferry Lane on the left. There is a marker at the entrance. This is the road that Burgoyne's forces marched on their way to a Boston prison camp.

Schuyler's Headquarters – Just a little further up US Route 4 is the Dirck Swart House. There is a marker near this privately owned home. As Schuyler's Headquarters, this home was once the Headquarters of the Northern Department of the Continental Army.

Prior to Saratoga, Benedict Arnold was dispatched from this house to put a stop to the British advance on

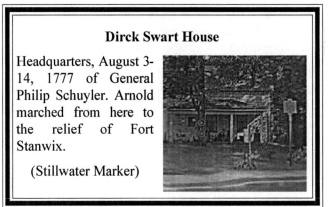

Dirck Swart House

Headquarters, August 3-14, 1777 of General Philip Schuyler. Arnold marched from here to the relief of Fort Stanwix.

(Stillwater Marker)

133

Montressor's Blockhouse and Storehouse Barracks, 1758, Fort Winslow, 1756, Schuyler's Supply Depot, 1777.

(Stillwater Marker)

Albany from the west. Burgoyne had hoped that the British would capture Albany from three directions, north, south and west. Stillwater was as close as they got from the north, Kingston from the south and Fort Stanwix from the west. The advance from the west began at Fort Ontario and was stalled at Fort Stanwix. Fortunately, the size of Arnold's forces was greatly amplified by the poor communication systems of the day. The British forces withdrew and Arnold returned.

Across from the Dirck Swart House is General Schuyler Lane. At this intersection, there is a marker listing the many historical sites that were once here, including Schuyler's supply depot.

Stillwater Blockhouse – Continuing down US Route 4, you will come to a blockhouse in the river park near the Hudson River. A marker on the blockhouse is a lamentation that the people of Stillwater have always

> But Stillwater is proud of the fact (though deprived of the name) that here was purchased the liberty which shall endure when monuments have crumbled.
>
> (Stillwater Marker)

had about their place in history. Saratoga Springs is mistakenly thought of as the place where the Battles of Saratoga took place. Yet, Saratoga Springs is over ten

miles from Stillwater, where the battles did take place.

Schuyler Mansions – Just past the blockhouse is a Knox Trail marker and two markers that identify

Site of the Schuyler Mansion

Home of Rensselaer Schuyler, son of General Philip Schuyler.

(Stillwater Marker)

135

Schuyler homes. At the Hermanus Schuyler Mansion, George Washington was entertained during his inspection of the area near the end of the Revolutionary War. He also visited the Smythe House at Fort Edward during the same time period. Governor George Clinton and General Philip Schuyler ac-  companied Washington during his inspection.

136

STILLWATER TO WATERFORD

Mile Mark 141.1 – Depart Stillwater.

Mile Mark 142.4 – Pass under the Train Bridge on the west bank of the Hudson with the river clearly visible to the left. The river gets very wide here due to a dam that at one time provided waterpower. There is a lock off to the left to get around the dam.

You soon will travel between some very large factory buildings that look like they've been hit by a tornado. Actually they have. This area was struck in the spring of 1998. Much of the damage has been repaired but much remains.

Mile Mark 143.4 – Continue through the light and get into the left lane. Turn left and continue to follow US Route 4 through Mechanicville.

Mile Mark 144.7 – Take the exit to the left and continue south on US Route 4.

Mile Mark 149.8 – On the left is the Champlain Canal Lock #1. There is actually one more lock on the Hudson – the Federal Lock in Troy, NY. Once you get to

---

Champlain Canal Lock #1

(US Route 4 Marker)

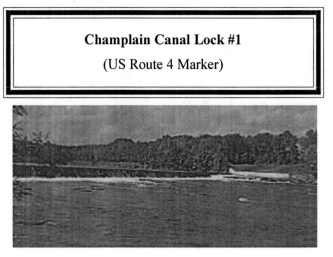

the other side of that lock, the Hudson River has essentially reached sea level. The river has a clear path all the way from Troy to New York City, some 140 miles.

Mile Mark 150.1 – Travel through the General Electric Plastics Plant. General Electric, which at one time had a very large presence in the area, has caused tremendous economic struggle with major labor reductions. The reductions were necessary in order to compete internationally. As General Electric continues to leave the area, they leave behind a history of dumping into the Hudson River. The river is much improved today, but PCB's that are buried in the soil along the banks remain an environmental concern.

Mike Mark 152.2 – As you near the town of Waterford, there is a nice view down river. You can see the bridge that carries US Route 4 across the Hudson from Waterford.

Mike Mark 152.6 – Watch
for the intersection with Hudson Street. Detour left onto Hudson Street then make your second right onto Second Street. Arrive in Waterford.

WATERFORD

Eagle Tavern – As you travel down Second Street, there is an Eagle Tavern marker between two homes on the right. The tavern was a colonial watering hole.

A little further down and across US Route 4 is a marker on the left that briefly explains the origin of the town's name.

Waterford Battery – At the end of Second Street is an

Eagle Tavern Site

Site of the colonial Eagle Tavern, a leading haven of area rebels during the American Revolution and operated by Gerardus Schoonhoven. Famous guests included Alexander Hamilton, Thomas Jefferson and James Madison.

(Waterford Marker)

139

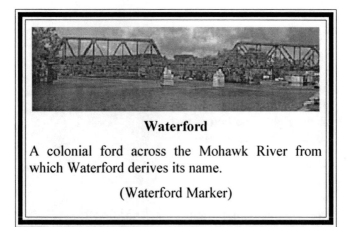

Waterford

A colonial ford across the Mohawk River from which Waterford derives its name.

(Waterford Marker)

area called "The Battery." It can be reached by bearing left at the old train bridge and squeezing between the bridge and a house. This area is also the location of the

The Battery

Site of an active 18th and 19th century river port considered the head of sloop navigation on the Hudson River between Waterford and New York City.

(Waterford Marker)

"water ford" that crossed the fourth branch of the Mohawk River to Peebles Island.

At the end of the battery area is a point where the Mohawk River first meets the Hudson River. This is also the point where both the Erie Canal and the Champlain Canal begin.

Memorial Park – Following First Street back to US Route 4, you will come to two parks along the Hudson River on each side of Route 4. In the park on the south side is another Knox Trail marker. When Knox reached Waterford in the winter of 1775-1776, he was delayed

141

because the ice was not thick enough to cross the Mohawk River. After drilling holes in the ice and allowing water to flow over the top to thicken it, he was able to continue his mission to Boston.

In the park on the north side of US Route 4 is a marker about Waterford's past.

WATERFORD TO PEEBLES ISLAND

Mile Mark 153.4 – Depart Waterford on the bridge across US Route 4. After the bridge, you will reach a light. The route is not marked very well here. Bear right.

Mile Mark 153.9 – Detour right onto 123rd Street and follow the street all the way until it dead-ends at the Hudson River. Directly across the river, you can see Peebles Island, the beginning of both the Erie Canal and Champlain Canal and Waterford.

Reverse direction and go back to US Route 4.

Mile Mark 154.8 – Follow US Route 4 south. Watch for the Olde 499 House on the right. The inn was originally an early Dutch house built in 1760. It was later became a stage coach stop between  Stockbridge, Massachusetts and Saratoga Springs and after that a bordello. Today, it is a popular restaurant.

Mile Mark 155.0 – Continue south until you reach the light on 112th Street in Troy. Detour right onto 112th Street and cross the bridge over the Hudson River. Take your first right after the bridge onto Delaware Avenue and follow Delaware Avenue until it ends at a park on Peebles Island.

Arrive at Peebles Island.

Peebles Island

In 1668, Philip Pietersen Schuyler and Goosen Gerritsen von Schaick acquired Peebles and van Schaick Islands and used the rich flood plain for planting crops and other areas for grazing cattle.

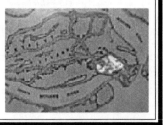

(Peebles Island Marker)

PEEBLES ISLAND

Peebles Island is surrounded by rivers. On the east side of the island is the Hudson River. On the north side is the fourth branch of the Mohawk River. On the west and south side is the third branch of the Mohawk River.

But despite its surroundings, the old military road from Fort Ann to Albany runs right though the middle of it. At the north end of the island, the road became the ford

On August 17, 1777, Americans retreated south to these islands. They prepared defenses to make a final stand against the British who intended to capture Albany. An American victory at Saratoga, however, made it unnecessary to rely upon the island's defenses. The fortifications consisted of three batteries of cannon protected by earth works all connected by entrenchments for troops. Their design has been attributed to Polish engineer, Thaddeus Kosciuszko.

(Peebles Island Marker)

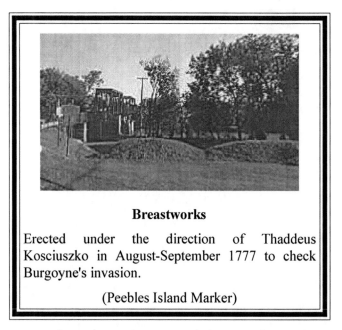

Breastworks

Erected under the direction of Thaddeus Kosciuszko in August-September 1777 to check Burgoyne's invasion.

(Peebles Island Marker)

across the water to battery park in Waterford, where you just visited.

There are several markers that provide the history of Peebles Island. During the Revolution, the island was prepared for a final stand against the British if they had won a victory at Saratoga.

PEEBLES ISLAND TO ALBANY

Mile Mark 156.1 – From the park, turn back on Delaware Avenue and follow the road back to 112th Street. Go straight across the intersection and continue down Delaware Avenue.

Mile Mark 157.3 – Turn right at Van Schaick road. The van Schaick home is near the corner of Van

---

Van Schaick Home

Home of John G. van Schaick and his wife Anna, patriot Americans. Built by Anthony van Schaick, son of Goosen Gerritsen van Schaick, original patentee. Headquarters, August 18 - September 8, 1777, Northern Department of the Continental Army. General Philip Schuyler and General Horatio Gates here planned the Saratoga campaign and here, August 19, 1777, General Gates assumed command. From this place, August 15, 1777, General Benedict Arnold and his force marched to relieve Fort Stanwix. Beneath this roof were received Governor George Clinton, General Benjamin Lincoln, General Ebenezer Learned, Colonel Peter Gansevoort, General Enoch Poor, General John Stark, Colonel Daniel Morgan, Colonel Thaddeus Kosciuszko, engineer of the fortifications on Peebles Island and at Bemis Heights. Here, also, after the surrender, were entertained General John Burgoyne and his staff.

(Peebles Island Marker)

Built in 1735, the van Schaick House located near the intersection of van Schaick and Delaware Avenue on van Schaick Island was probably used by Generals Haratio Gates and Philip Schuyler as headquarters for the northern department of the colonial army between August 18th and September 8, 1777. The Revolutionary War emphasized the strategic location of Peebles and van Schaick Islands. During the major British offensive of 1777 when General John Burgoyne was advancing from Montreal in an attempt to capture Albany, the islands were garrisoned by Americans who built extensive earthen fortifications along the northern edge of Peebles Island.

(Peebles Island Marker)

Schaick road and Delaware Ave. Like the Dirck Swart house in Stillwater, this home was also the headquarters of the Northern Department of the Continental Army. The marker lists the many people who have visited the home and reads like a *Who's Who at Saratoga*. The home is currently owned by the Daughters of the American Revolution.

Mile Mark 157.5 – Continue down van Schaick road to the stop sign and look for the military road marker

Military Road, from 1690 through the Revolution. Used by General Ebenezer Learned on his way to relieve Fort Stanwix, August 14, 1777.

(Peebles Island Marker)

> ### Camp Van Schaick
>
> Encampment of the Northern Department Continental Army, August 9 - September 8, 1777. From this place, August 9, 1777, Gen. Ebenezer Learned with his Massachusetts brigade marched to relieve Fort Stanwix.
>
> Erected by the Cohoes Historical Society and the State of New York, 1928.
>
> (Van Schaick Marker)

on the right. There is another reference to Fort Stanwix on the marker.

Just past the stop sign is a park on the right with two Camp Van Schaick markers. Camp Van Schaick was a staging area for Fort Stanwix and Saratoga.

Turn left after the park then right on Bridge Avenue.

Mile Mark 158.1 – Reach the intersection with Route 787. Continue through the intersection until you reach the intersection with Route 32. Turn left onto Route 32 going south. You will complete your **Revolutionary Day** on Route 32 to Albany.

> ### Camp Van Schaick
>
> Continental Army, Northern Department under command of General Philip Schuyler, General Horatio Gates, August 15 - September 8, 1777.
>
> (Peebles Island Marker)

Mile Mark 160.3 – Enter the town of Watervliet.

Mile Mark 160.8 – Reach 19th Street. On your left is the 19th Street Bridge, which crosses the Hudson. From the bridge, you get a nice view of the city of Troy. Be warned, however, if you take the bridge, the lanes split onto one-way streets in Troy. You will have to go around a couple blocks to get back.

Mile Mark 161.2 – Turn left onto 13th Street following Route 32 south.

Mile Mark 161.4 – Turn right at the next light onto Broadway following Route 32 South.

Mile Mark 161.6 – Watch for the Watervliet Arsenal on the right. The arsenal is the oldest, continually

active manufacturing arsenal in the United States, founded in 1813. The museum contains a collection of howitzers, naval guns and artillery used throughout the history of the United States. Amongst the artillery is "George the 2nd," a British 24 Pounder. This is one of two 24 Pounders that were surrendered by the British at the Battle of Saratoga. The museum is open to the public, Monday-Thursday, 10am-3pm.

Mile Mark 164.2 – Continue south on Route 32 through the town of Menands.

Mile Mark 164.9 – Go under Interstate 90.

Mile Mark 165.3 – Depart from Route 32 and stay on Broadway into the city of Albany.

Mile Mark 166.1 – Watch for "Nipper" the dog on top of a building on the left. Nipper is the famous RCA dog that listens to "his master's voice."

Mile Mark 167.0 – Go under the train bridge used by Amtrak's Lake Shore Limited to Chicago.

Mile Mark 167.2 – As you near the center of Albany, watch for Quackenbush Square on the left.

Arrive in Albany.

Quackenbush House – In Quackenbush Square is the Quackenbush house and the Albany Visitor Center. The house is the former home of Hendrick Quackenbush, an officer who served in the Revolutionary War. After Saratoga, Quackenbush was responsible for the

Quackenbush House

Circa 1730, the oldest existing structure in the city of Albany. The house is considered to be one of the finest remaining examples of Dutch urban architecture in this country. The original stepped front gable was modified to its present federal style when the house was expanded around 1790 by Colonel Hendrique Quackenbush, who inherited the home from his father. Colonel Quackenbush was the leader of Albany's 5th Military Regiment which fought against Burgoyne's army at Saratoga in 1777. The house remained connected to the Quackenbush-Lansing family until after the American Civil War.

(Albany Marker)

prisoner, General John Burgoyne, and it is believed that he was a prisoner/guest at the house. Today, it is the oldest house in Albany and is currently the home of Nicole's Bistro, a very popular local restaurant.

Albany Visitor Center – Next to the Quackenbush House is the Albany Visitor Center. In the center are many exhibits that cover the history of Albany. They include many old drawings and maps of Albany from the Revolutionary War period as well as periods before and after. At the center, you can pick up a pamphlet entitled, "Capital City! A Walking Tour." The complete tour is recommended on a longer visit to the area.

The Tricentenial Park – Diagonally across the street from Quackenbush Square is Tricentenial Park. The park was built in 1986 and commemorates Albany's 300th anniversary from 1686.

Fort Frederick
Albany Visitor Center Exhibit

First Church in Albany – Diagonally across from Tricentennial Park is First Church. Inside is the oldest pulpit and weathercock in America brought from the Church of Amsterdam in 1656. On top of the building is a replica of the weathercock, bullet holes and all.

Fort Frederick – In 1777, Fort Frederick was target-center for the British invasion. The site of Fort Frederick can be reached by heading past First Church on Broadway and turning right on Pine Street to Eagle Street. There are several markers on Eagle Street near the State Capitol. One of the markers is a ground marker near the road. Fort Frederick was built by the British in 1675.

> Facing the river on an eminence in this broad street, opposite St. Peter's Church stood Fort Frederick. Built about 1676, removed in 1784, Callows Hill to the south, fort burial ground to the north.
>
>
>
> (Albany Marker)

City Hall – City Hall is at the intersection with Eagle Street. In front of City Hall is a statue of General Philip Schuyler. Although the statue depicts a stern, strong and triumphant Schuyler, it is often characterized as "brooding" — this, in reference to his failed invasion of Canada in 1776, the loss of Fort Ticonderoga in 1777 and his replacement by General Horatio Gates as Commander of the Northern Department of the Continental Army prior to the battles of Saratoga.

> In the middle of this street to the east stood Fort Frederick, goal of Burgoyne's drive to split the colonies in 1777.
>
> (Albany Marker)

Schuyler was later vindicated by Congress and should be remembered more for his ability in building and supplying the army's Northern Department. The British retreated twice from the army that he built, once at Fort Ticonderoga and Mount Independence in 1776 and again at Saratoga in 1777.

Just up the street from City Hall heading west is a highway marker. The marker highlights Albany's place as a crossroad. During the Revolution, military roads ran north, south, east and west from Albany. Today, interstates, US highways and railroads do the same as well as the waterways that run west, north and south.

The Schuyler Mansion – Philip Schuyler's Revolutionary War home is a state historic site preserved on the southeast side of the city. The house can be reached by following Eagle Street past the capitol (get into the far right lane in front of the capitol building), the Egg (a very large sculpture that contains two back-to-back theatres), the Corning Tower, the Cathedral of the Immaculate Conception and the Governor's Mansion.

Directional signs will help you make the left turn on Morton Street and the right on Clinton Street.

Just up Clinton Street on the right is the Schuyler Mansion. Parking is available behind the mansion, which is open Wednesday-Saturday, 10am-5pm, Sunday, 1-5pm. The small carriage house near the mansion is the Visitor Center. You are instructed to ring the bell for a tour, which is recommended on a longer visit to the area.

Schuyler Mansion
by Philip Hooker

Schuyler Mansion, built in the early 1760's, was the prominent feature of an estate of approximately 80 acres. Several other buildings, many involved with the operation of Schuyler's farm, as well as two wings adjacent to the house, also occupied the grounds. This view shows the main house in 1818 when it was owned by John Bryan. One of the wings and Schuyler's large Dutch barn appear at the right of the house. The vestibule on the front of the house was added after Schuyler's death in 1804.

(Albany Marker)

Schuyler Mansion

Erected 1762. The home of Major General Philip Schuyler of the American Revolution. Patriot, soldier, statesman. 1733-1804.

(Albany Marker)

There are two markers at the front of the house, one at the approach to the front door of the mansion and another at the top of the steps.

Burgoyne was also a prisoner/guest at the Schuyler Mansion. He stayed here with his 20-member staff for ten days before moving on to Boston. During that time, he and his staff enjoyed the hospitality of Philip Schuyler's wife, Catherine Van Rensselaer Schuyler.

Alexander Hamilton and the Schuylers' daughter, Elizabeth were engaged in March 1780. Their marriage took place at the mansion in December of the same year. Alexander Hamilton served under George Washington as his Aide-de-Camp and trusted advisor for four and a half years. After his marriage in July 1781, he served under Lafayette and participated in the siege at Yorktown.

Also in the summer of 1781, the Schuyler Mansion was attacked by a band of Tories. The attackers attempted to take Schuyler prisoner, but he was prepared for the attack and fought them off from his bedroom. To this day, there is a hatchet mark on the stairway banister that resulted from a thrown tomahawk during the attack.

In December 1780, the Marquis de Chastellux wrote: "A handsome house, halfway up the bank opposite the ferry, seems to attract the eye and to invite strangers to stop at General Schuyler's who is its owner as well as its architect. I had recommendations to him from all quarters, but particularly from General Washington and Mrs. Carter, Schuyler's daughter. On shore was the Chevalier de Mauduit, who was waiting for us with the General's sleigh and found ourselves in an instant in a handsome drawing room near a good fire with Mr. Schuyler, his wife and daughter.

While we were warming ourselves, dinner was served to which everyone did honor as well as to the Madiera which was excellent and which made us completely forget the rigor of the season and the fatigue of the journey."

(Albany Marker)

Overnight in Albany – A nearby spot for the evening is the Mansion Hill Inn and Restaurant. The inn is a downtown bed and breakfast not far from the Schuyler Mansion. It features a small number of comfortable rooms and an award winning restaurant. The inn is just a block east of the Governor's Mansion on Philip Street. Reservations are recommended (888-299-0455).

BIBLIOGRAPHY

Bobrick, Benson, **Angel in the Whirlwind,** Penguin Books, New York, 1997.

Hamilton, Edward P., **Fort Ticonderoga, Key to a Continent,** Little, Brown and Company, Boston, 1964.

Mintz, Max M., **The Generals of Saratoga, John Burgoyne and Horatio Gates,** Yale University Press, New Haven, 1990.

National Park Service, US Department of the Interior, "Saratoga", GPO: 1997-417-648/60107, 1997.

Purcell, L. Edward and David F. Burg, Editors, **The World Almanac of the American Revolution,** Pharos Books, New York, 1992.

Vermont Division for Historic Preservation, "Hubbardton Battlefield State Historic Site", 1996.

Vermont Division for Historic Preservation, "Mount Independence, State Historic Site", 1997.

Raymond C. Houghton is a freelance historian and sole proprietor of Cyber Haus of Delmar, NY. He is a retired college professor, former government bureaucrat, Vietnam Veteran and one-time, General Electric employee. He has honors from the Department of Commerce, is listed in Who's Who in America and holds a doctorate from Duke University.